The Scent of Jasmine

Library of Congress Cataloging-in-Publication Data

Gatto, Florence Terranova, 1939-
  The scent of jasmine : vignettes from a Sicilian heritage / Florence Terranova Gatto.
    p. cm.
  ISBN 1-881901-62-9 (pbk.)
  1. Gatto, Florence Terranova, 1939- 2. Italian Americans—New York (State)—New York—Biography. 3. Italian Americans—New York (State)—New York—Social life and customs. 4. New York (N.Y.)—Biography. I. Title.
  F128.9.I8G37 2007
  974.7'1004510092—dc22
  [B]

                            2007041100

Acknowledgements
The publisher is grateful to Arba Sicula for a generous grant that in part made the publication of this book possible.

The publisher is grateful to Giulia Di Filippi for the use of her oil painting for the cover. Giulia Di Filippi is an Italian artist from Isernia, Molise.

For information and for orders, write to:

Legas

P.O. Box 149
Mineola, NewYork
11501, USA

3 Wood Aster Bay
Ottawa, Ontario
K2R 1D3 Canada

legaspublishing.com
PRINTED IN CANADA

Florence Terranova Gatto

The Scent of Jasmine:

Vignettes from a Sicilian Heritage

LEGAS

With eternal love for my children Lorraine, John, Kenneth, and Steven and for the grandchildren they gave me.

Acknowledgements

Most of the essays presented in this collection have appeared in the NYS OSIA Golden Lion newspaper edited by Salvatore Moschella. He has guided many essays into coherent pieces for the column "Then and Now". I extend thanks to OSIA for the opportunity to share my love for the Italian heritage. The essays depict true personal experiences, as I recall them.

I extend grateful thanks to members of the Long Island Writers Guild for support, suggestions, and motivation. Blessings to Peter Garenani, founder of the LIWG, for his instruction and inspiration in making me an author.

I am indebted to Alyson Kendric, Francesca Magliochetti, Frank Prestigiacomo, Jean Nisi, and Nancy and Vincent Romano for comments, suggestions, and patience in reading unedited pieces. Special thanks to my sisters Anne and Katherine and cousin Caterine who sometimes recall different aspects of the same incident and who respectfully defer to the writer!

To Gaetano Cipolla, whose passion for Sicily is contagious, for his unending patience during the publication of this book, thank you.

Although many stories are based on experiences of growing up in an Italian immigrant household, others can identify with the universality of the situations and the sentiments portrayed.

Finally, I hope my children and grandchildren will enjoy my stories and learn from my memoirs. My wish is that they visit and remember always, their heritage and the land of their ancestors where "1' odore di gelsomino" is rampant.

Table of *Contents*

The Women (in America)

The Holidays (in America)

Preface

When I was a child, the sweet smell of jasmine on my terrace was intoxicating. I believe nature's gift to the world is the scent of flowers and the delicate jasmine blossom has one of the most distinctive, potent, unforgettable, and beautiful aromas. I am convinced that the sweet jasmine blossoms were the catalyst that piqued my curiosity about Italy and made me an Italophile.

My father cultivated a fragile sprig of jasmine sent from Villabate, his town in Sicily, with the innate skill of a horticulturist. That plant was a reminder of a home he knew he would not return to for a long time. He nurtured the delicate cutting with enriched soil, water, and daily care. I recognized the signs of nostalgia as he explained the exotic Asian origin of the plant, the need for warm climate, and how the fragrance was entwined with gentle breezes in Italy. Jasmine grows and blooms in abundance in Sicily, on sides of houses, around railings, in crevices of the Greek and Roman ruins, and wherever it can root itself. My father cared for the young plant as a symbol of loyalty to his birthplace and also as a romantic devotion to my mother.

My mother loved the soothing perfume created by the star shaped flowers. In the evening she would pinch some of the fine stems and put them in a small vial before a blessed statue on a bureau. The bouquet permeated the bedroom. The sweet night scent from the tiny flowers was also captured in a sachet and placed between embroidered linens.

My mother's natural perfume was from a few delicate white blossoms she placed in her cleavage. The scent wafted from her body temperature and the whiff of jasmine surrounded her like an aura. To this day I associate jasmine scent with my mother.

My grandmother, a gifted storyteller, knew folklore tales about everything. Most of them had a spiritual moral. The one about jasmine always remained a lasting memory:

"Mary, Mother of Jesus was going through a guard post cradling her infant Son. A gruff guard asked her,

'What do you have in your arms?'

Mary, trembling with fright whispered, 'Gesu Mio.' to which the stern guard said, 'Let me see.'

9

Mary opened her cape and miraculously in the folds of her garment was a profusion of white fragrant flower stars. The gathers of her robe were overflowing with small clusters of live petals like jewels in the sun: *gelsomino*.

'Only jasmine' announced the guard, 'Let her through'.

'Gesu Mio became "Gelsomino" so similar in Italian pronunciation. So the miracle of jasmine saved Mary and Baby Jesus from the guards and harm."

While our garden provided fresh herbs and special food needs such as fennel fronds, and zucchini blossoms, our revered jasmine plant was different. Gelsomino was cultivated for nourishment of the soul, the nostalgic Sicilian soul that laments the displacement from the ancestral home, but prevails, survives, and recalls the history, tradition, and beauty of the Sicilian island.

Now I tend to a jasmine plant on my patio and the tradition continues. I anticipate the tiny pink tinged buds blossoming into a purity of white flowers whose scent will remind me of long ago.

The invoking fragrance reminds me of events in my life, the humor in some home practices and of immigrant families in the neighborhood linking two worlds.

To my astonishment, jasmine weaves itself into my life again. My son's home in Califonia is jasmine scented by a trellis covered with the same variety of jasmine that we had years ago.

"I love these flowers, Mom. They smell great at night."

"I know." I smile.

"Water them well." I advise.

I wonder, "Are these sweet jasmine blossoms his Nonno reincarnate?"

"Will the gelsomino be the thread that weaves our generations together?Is the Sicilian soul vying for recognition and preservation?"

I explain my connection and love for the flowering vine and silently designate gelsomino as a guardian of my family's heritage.

Led by the strong perfume of fragile blossoms dear reader, I write these fond memoirs and share them with you.

The Italians (in America)

The Italians in America stories depict the difficulties of transition for the immigrants, their adjustment, and ultimately their comfort in the new land. Appropriately my name Terranova, translates to new land. For years I joked that I should be called Miss America. The anecdotes chronicle my observations of relatives and friends as they became Americans.

The cousins picnic on the rocks.

Tangerine orchards in Sicily.

THE ITALOPHILE

I'm an Italophile! I love Italy! How did that happen? Maybe my grandmother's stories about the sweet night scents of Jasmine and Zagara, or the fanciful Sicilian cart adorned with colorful plumes in the bakery window piqued my interest. But when I learned about the Renaissance and the genius of Da Vinci I knew I had to go to Italy. There were no third year college abroad programs in my day, so the next best thing was to get married and go to Italy on a honeymoon!

After a visit to the enchanting Medici city of Florence, a gondola ride in Venice, an audience with Pope John XXIII and surviving the Amalfi drive, we made a dutiful visit to my parent's hometown. The anticipation, desire, and reality of arriving in Italy all blended as I walked down the metal steps of the plane onto the tarmac of Palermo airport. A symphony of greetings shattered the years of photograph familiarity and reassembled as three dimensions of swarming cousins I didn't know I had. A huge bouquet of flowers was thrust into my hands and my cheeks became rosy from the friction of a zillion kisses.

Until then, only retiree went back to the paese. As a newlywed in the Kennedy era, I arrived with a flowered hat, gloves, and high-heeled shoes, so I was treated like a movie star. We were pressed into a mini Fiat 500 and giggled all the way to town in the sweltering heat of July.

The first walk through the piazza, an entourage, arm in arm led us to say "Buon giorno" to my grandparents- albeit, posthumously, - at the cemetery! They were long gone and I was the only grandchild they had never met. This was a strategic plan. The relatives wanted me to learn about my ancestors and trace my roots. What better place than the cemetery? I looked at the picture inserts on the gravestones, placed a flower in a vase, and immediately understood the continuity of family and ties to the old country. My uncle still lived in the small house my father was born in. It was a real house with bedrooms upstairs, an open fire kitchen and bathroom downstairs, with sporadic water in those days. There were a few chickens in the yard to provide fresh eggs, I think! We went to the tangerine and olive orchards and ate berries from the trees. Then we went on tour, house to house, to meet relatives. Not to slight anyone, we ate

13

identical meals twice a day. *Pasta al pomodoro, insalata, un po' di carne, frutta*, and *vino, vino, vino*. Then came the after dinner circle and questions about everything from movies to politics. The young people craved to hear a contemporary viewpoint of life in New York. They knew more than I did about our government. Some of it propaganda, but at least it was an interest. They laughed at the antiquated words we used. The time spent with the relatives was unforgettable. The people and place entered my heart forever.

They say you must know where you are coming from to know where you are going. My relatives taught me where I came from and I knew I would be going back to Italy many many times. I did not know I would have to wait twenty-two years with a tarantella in my head. Then the United States government gave me a teacher grant. I fled without my family to immerse myself in my love for Italy. I had a view of the Etruscan Arch from my classroom in Perugia and a few years later with another study grant I lived in a villa in Siena with a view of sunflowers and vineyards. It was hard to believe it was not a dream. Now whenever I go to Italy, I feel as though I am going home. A trip to Italy is like taking vitamins for me. I get a boost of energy and feel, alert, creative, and alive there. The first thing I do is buy new shoes: I develop a bounce to my step over the ancient cobblestones as I attempt to cross the streets in Rome. I lament about the value of the Euro and buy a handbag anyway. I try a different flavor of *gelato* every day. I walk faster, laugh louder, and breathe better. I smile while I am there and shed a tear as I leave. I had the opportunity of sharing my enthusiasm about Italy when I escorted teenagers on tours. But my greatest desire is to introduce my grandchildren to the little boot in the Mediterranean that has delectable cuisine, painted ceilings, fast cars, great fashions, music in the streets, folklore festivals, almond blossoms, huge lemons, and the relatives!

I propose an obligatory trip to Italy for every young person. A short visit will provide a visual point of reference and put into perspective world history. They could develop self esteem and a sense of pride for the rich and respected culture that is our heritage. There is history and beauty everywhere. Just by visiting the ruins of the Roman Empire, art museums, and the Vatican, the intellectual growth can be savored for the rest of their lives. They might like the rhythm of the Italian day- awakened by church bells, pranzo at one o'clock, little nap after that, passeggiata, conversation and caffe', and become an Italophile like me!

Although my allegiance is red, white, and blue, my heart and blood are red, white, and green! What a wonderful combination. I feel exceptionally blessed that my ancestors came from *bella Italia*.

Then honeymoon,

now nonna.

THE PIANOLA

My grandmother arrived in New York in 1920 with two children and a mandolin among her treasured possessions. Apparently she had no intention of living in America without music. The strong tradition of music and song was carried across the Atlantic by the multitude of Italian immigrants and produced a legacy of famous entertainers that continues to shape American culture

One of the earliest purchases when the family had settled on the lower East side of Manhattan was a shiny black upright piano.

My sister took piano lessons and played well. My first piano teacher was "Professore Panza." With a big belly and dyed hair, he was a serious musician; I was not. The next teacher was a young woman who terrorized me into one hour of daily practice of Hanon, Czerny and Streborg before I could play any familiar melody. After "Twinkle Twinkle" my first memorized piece was "Torna a Sorrento," an easy version. I was not expected to become a concert pianist but I was certainly obliged to demonstrate my talent (or lack of) to visitors on Sunday afternoon. I can still hear .

"Vai, vai, suona una mazurka."

I played as loud as I could. Later as a teenager I had the freedom to buy sheet music of movie themes or Broadway shows. I learned to read my first Italian words from the sheet music. The directions *fortissimo, crescendo, piano, adagio, lentamente* etc. (Everybody knew I particularly liked *fortissimo*.)

What I couldn't play I pumped out of the pianola. The old upright had a lower hidden compartment that contained oversized pedals and a smaller niche above the ivory keys where perforated parchment piano rolls were placed into the player piano. I was curious so I would open the doors to expose the innards of the piano. I would watch in amazement as the keys flew up and down and the hammers hit the strings, all activated by my pumping and the perforated parchment rolling over some cylinders(much like a music box). Slow pumping changed the melody and tempo of the music and my cousins and I had lots of fun pumping vigorously speeding up the opera arias and four hand arrangements. We tried to follow the notes with my own fingers.

The music rolls, imported from Italy, came in foot long boxes that were labeled at one end with the name of the performer and usually were stored on the piano itself. Words to the songs were also written on some of the rolls in script.

Later when it was not fashionable to have a pianola the mechanism was removed and the precious piano rolls were relegated to a barrel in the cellar. Unfortunately some musical mice munched on the sweet notes and destroyed what probably would have been collector's items today.

So before CDs, DVDs, Tvs, and videos we had entertainment, LIVE ENTERTAINMENT by members of the family who were active rather than passive participants in the music.

We probably remember someone in our family who played an accordion, violin, guitar, mandolin or even a jew's harp. A jam session and sing along created an immediate festive atmosphere. I tried to perpetuate the musical tradition. My sons played in the school band in the brass section and my daughter plays piano and violin.

Sadly my grandmother's mandolin is history and if we ever find it among the cellar or attic treasures we will probably hang it on the wall as a symbol of our heritage.

VINO

The East end of Long Island is glorious in the fall, especially the North Fork. I recently spent a weekend pumpkin picking and visiting the vineyards in Peconic. When I entered one winery it looked like a science lab with stainless steel machinery. At a long bar young ladies poured wine into small glasses for the visitors to sample. The wines produced there had names such as Winter White, Summer Blush, Merlot, Cabernet Noir etc.

THEN, I recalled my own personal wine tasting sessions when I was growing up in Brooklyn. My father's wine was called "vino" although at times we had "moscato". My father made his own wine in the cellar. I remember the scent of crushed grape permeating the entire house the days in early November when it was wine time. Every member of the family was expected to help in the process. Barrels were cleaned using burning sulfur sticks and hot water in preparation for the new vintage. I went with my father onto the freight trains that brought the grapes from California. I remember my father tasting a few grapes to see if the sugar content was to his liking. He knew nothing of "ph factors". The grapes were crushed (not with our feet but a hand turned masher), fermented, and put in wooden presses that were imported from Italy. We took turns at cranking the wine press and it was more difficult as the grapes became drier. A deep purple liquid dripped out of the press into a basin, then was poured into barrels to age in the cold wine room of the cellar. After the wine aged a few months, we had our own private wine tasting and competition. Every neighbor would brag that his wine was the best and a challenge was on the way. Sometimes relatives brought samples of their wines when they visited. There was always a discussion as to whose wine was stronger, which color was clearer, which was more fragrant. We didn't know enough to look for legs on the glass. We didn't even use stemware. We used a short juice type glass. My father's wine was always the best. If a barrel was exceptionally good, a few bottles were saved for special occasions such as weddings or baptisms.

The tailor across the street made wine too but each year my mother sent me there to buy vinegar! So my father made the best wine and the tailor made great "wine vinegar" for our salads. Every night the wine bottle was filled straight from the barrel and brought

18

to the dinner table. It was always chilled perfectly. We all drank wine with our meals but I never saw anyone drunk in my family. We even dunked bread in wine to help soothe our teething babies. In summer we had peaches in wine or sometimes mixed a little soda in the glass- a wine spritzer!

Later, as I sat on the veranda of the winery listening to the musicians play bluegrass music, I watched the silvery leaves on the vines sway in the gentle breeze. It was reminiscent of the vineyards in Tuscany and Sicily. I thought, if only my father had known that grapes could grow on the East end of Long Island. If only he had been told "Go East young immigrant." He would have been a great wine maker and the music on the veranda might have been a mandolin playing a Sicilian tarantella.

Robert Lewis Stevenson said,"Wine is bottled poetry." I guess my father was a poet!

EVERYONE TO THE HAMPTONS

Follow any Land Rover on the Long Island parkways and it will probably lead you to East, South, West, Bridge Hampton or perhaps Hampton Bays. It seems the sun energizes the mass exodus from the city. The Hamptons are definitely the "in" place right now.

When I visit family and friends out there I am tempted to ask my hosts, "Does Martha Stewart live here with you?"

The summer houses are perfectly decorated in bright colors, with leather couches, matching pillows, floral dishes, tinted stem ware, and tiled floors. They have skylights, stainless steel barbecues, landscaped gardens, an organic vegetable patch, and of course a heated swimming pool!

What a difference from the way I spent my summers years ago. I went to Coney Island and attended the school playground program. The only place our vintage Buick took us was across the river to New Jersey for the highlight of the summer: a visit to "the lots." Many immigrants bought lots with the hope of building a dream house on it someday. Every year a physical examination of the land was made to see that there was no infringement of the property and to reenforce the dream. We ate our homemade sandwiches on the grass, sitting among the insects. Searching out the newest restaurant in town was unheard of. Sometimes an improvised barbecue was constructed with two cinder blocks and a small grate over a wood fire for a quick grilling of a thin steak. Of course we did not go antiquing. After all my relatives had recently made the trip from the ultimate antique area of all, Italy. We called those stores "junk stores" and now the junk costs a lot of money.

I was allowed to spend a few weeks with my cousins at their grandmother's farm upstate in Highland, New York. It was a working dairy farm and we were the workers. My cousins were up at the crack of dawn to milk the cows. My job was to feed the chickens. I was afraid of them so I'd stamp my feet when I entered the chicken coop and scattered the entire contents of the feed pail at the clucking hens and roosters and ran out as fast as I could.

The old farmhouse was also a guest house but guests were limited to *paesani*. Each family was allowed to use the kitchen and had an assigned table in one of the sunny alcoves of the dining room. Everyone shared a bathroom and the kids were told to use the outhouse. Evenings were for card playing or sitting on the Adirondack chairs telling stories, risquè jokes or singing.

During the day the kids romped through the fields and collected wild flowers or weeds with pods that popped when pressed between two fingers. We had a Norman Rockwell swing-an old tire on a rope-that entertained us during the sunset hours. Our swimming pool was the dug out area of the cool, running brook on the property.

We didn't have skylights in the old Victorian house but we did have starlight when we sat on the wraparound porch in the evening. We took turns on the canvas hammock and listened to a portable radio if the batteries were not dead. We collected lightning bugs, that we put in jars and kept beside our beds as night lights.

We had to pump water, but oh what water it was, cold, sweet, spring water that is probably being bottled and sold in our supermarkets now.

Later when Italian Americans became more "affluent" and we rented or bought small cottages in the country, they collected the household discards all winter for "the summer house". Chipped dishes, faded linens, old pots all were recycled to the summer place. One family used jelly jars as glasses. Martha would be appalled.

Now we have architects who create magnificent mansions on the beach and then we silence the sound of the crashing waves by air conditioning. We have boats and wet bikes, dishwashers, DVDs, everything; but where are the fireflies?

We've come a long way from a little place in the country, *una casa in campagna.*

I LOVE OPERA

Fall in New York means opera season to me. You either love opera or hate opera! Some people think it is screaming to music but I hear melodious tones that stir emotions. I follow the intricate plots of intrigue, betrayal, mistaken identity, and scenes of prolonged dying and I love it. Tickets for my opera series just arrived and I am looking forward to enjoying La Boehme at the Metropolitan again. I am thrilled that I saw Pavarotti perform in *Aida* and *Tosca,* and so sorry that I missed the era of that great Neapolitan tenor Enrico Caruso.

I did not always have the good fortune of going to grand opera. When I was in college, my friends and I identified with the bohemian Rodolfo and Mimi. When we had the opportunity to get FREE tickets for a little opera house on Bleecker Street in Greenwich Village, that was our Saturday night date!

The owner collected tickets and not only played the piano as the accompaniment for the singers but at intermission passed around the hat. That was Anthony Amato and the Amato Opera Company still exists in lower Manhattan. We "generously" gave a couple of dollars and saved the rest of our money for the coffee houses nearby. The creative sets at times appeared precarious, while aspiring singers of all sizes and shapes wore costumes that were re cycled. Once, Carmen's dress was so tight that it split as she sang a fiery aria! It took awhile to compose ourselves.

Since then I have seen opera "al fresco" in Verona with thousands in the audience holding lit candles during the overture at twilight. I'll never forget the outdoor extravaganza of *Aida* at the Baths of Caracalla in Rome either. Live elephants, camels and horses marched in triumph across the huge stage strewn with ancient ruins. The symphony orchestra was at times accompanied by clicking crickets in the heat of the spotlights.

When I traveled to Italy with students I felt obligated to introduce them to opera. They were more impressed with the snack bar. If they never go to an opera again, at least, they had one memorable evening at the Baths of Caracalla!

Equally thrilling was watching Gianni Schicchi in a piazza of a small town. I sat on the church steps(without a cushion) and enjoyed Puccini's sweet tones under a star studded Italian sky. The backdrop scenery was authentic and the audience seemed to understand every word.

The homes of composers are revered places in Italy. I visited the Rossini birthplace and museum in Pesaro and even sat on Puccini's piano bench in Lucca, but neither helped my musical talent. Not long ago I saw my parent's town, Villabate, listed in the program at the Metropolitan Opera. I couldn't believe that the baritone, Simone Alaimo, in the role of Barber of Seville and the lead voice in *La Cenerentola* came from Villabate, Sicily, the town where my cousins still live, but it was true! I was graciously invited backstage to meet the distant relative.

Opera houses in Italy reflect the elegance and formality of the music and are steeped in history. La Scala di Milano really has a beautiful staircase. La Fenice in Venice, and the San Carlo in Naples had debuts of major operas. After many years in restoration the majestic Teatro Massimo in Palermo now has performances. Opera is respected in Italy and at one time the theme from *Nabucco*, "Va pensiero" was considered for the national anthem.

Somehow the immigrants of the last century were exposed to opera stories and themes. Verdi and Puccini, having lived in the early 1900's were actually their contemporaries. NOW as I reminisce, I can thank the Amato Opera Company for the exposure and making opera lovers out of a bunch of silly teenagers. After the powerful opera finales I often stand, sigh, and shout, " Bravo."

Opera at the Baths of Caracalla, Rome.

SOCCER TIME

Italy's *Azzurri* are world champions! They won the coveted Soccer World Cup this summer only for the fourth time in history. The last time was in 1982. Italians are crazy for soccer and carry their passion wherever they go. The celebrations in the Italian American neighborhoods in New York were joyous and surpassed any celebration for American sport victories of Baseball World Series, Football Super Bowl, or Hockey Stanley Cup. I watched the final game between France and Italy last summer on television and rooted for Italy, of course. After a tied score of 1 to1, carried to the second half, and with overtime exhausted, the shootout of penalty kicks began. Those last seconds, when only one more point was needed to win, were tense. Even I, a tame sports fan, was emotionally involved and on edge.

Someone I know was quite ingenious. He was on the phone in his home in Brooklyn speaking to his cousin in Sicily and because of the 30 seconds delay in the television transmittal he knew the outcome of the kick point exactly 30 seconds before the American viewers. If I were the gambling sort, I could have placed a bet during those last seconds and made a fortune. I guess other people might think of that also.

When I was in school, soccer games were assigned the smaller field without bleachers. Not many boys were interested in the sport THEN. Only a few students newly arrived from foreign countries played. NOW there are soccer leagues everywhere in the suburbs and cities. My grandchildren, both girls and boys play on soccer teams as early as age four and love the sport.

Italian kids get soccer balls when they are toddlers. I see many young families in parks in Italy following a rolling soccer ball, guided by a little Italian foot, coached by a proud parent.

Così. Guarda. Vai, vai, dacci un calcio. Bravo, the father directs. The apparent 14-month-old smiles, having no words developed yet, often tumbles over the ball and giggles. Parents are hopeful that he may grow up to be one of the star players on a professional team some day.

I am elated that the World Cup championship will focus positive attention on Italy's favorite sport and I assume there will be many babies named Fabio, Alessandro and Andrea for those handsome winning athletes.

When I was teaching English as a Second language, my teenage students were allowed to go outside at lunchtime. In the afternoon, I tried to refocus the class, so a calming math assignment was usually waiting on the chalkboard. One day only half my class returned from lunch- mostly girls.

"Where are the rest of the boys?"

"Look out the window, Mrs. Gatto," they said. Expecting the worst I glanced at the park across the street and sure enough my students were engaged in a peaceful international encounter, a soccer game! My Russian, Italian, South American, Chinese and Polish students were safe and happy enough but lost track of time. With a call to the Principal's office, they were quickly rounded up by the Dean of Students and reprimanded in five languages.

I hope Italy can repeat the role of conquering heroes and return the glory to Rome again at the next World Cup in four years. *Forza Azzurri!*

NAMESAKES

Joy of all joys, I recently became a grandmother, in December and again in August, of two gorgeous baby girls! Is either one of them named after me? Not a chance! The names were also kept secret from me until the births!

This wouldn't have been the case years ago. Names were predetermined THEN by tradition and strict formula. There were no sleepless nights thinking of names to go with the surname, no anguish about an acronym forming with initials (such as Nunzio Ugo Terranova becoming NUT) and no choice for fear of rousing the ire of ancestors.

Precisely, the first born would be named after paternal grandparents and the second of the same gender for the maternal family and then alternating between families. The only slight deviation allowed was for a patron saint and even that was usually a middle name. When grandparents names were exhausted, aunts and uncles names were alternated down the family lines. It was very simple.

Ritualized at baptism the new namesake gave honor and respect to the saint and the person (who might not have been so saintly). Names had a masculine form and a feminine form. You were Domenica or Domenico, or Nicola or Nicoletta. In translation some of the names Elaria, Orazio, Sebastiano,(Hillary, Horace, Sebastian) weren't so bad but some purist grandparents protested. So Biaggio as Blaise or Girolama as Geraldine were unacceptable.

My family had three Caterinas, four Giuseppes, and three Antoninas, all named after the same people. My cousins in Italy are known as Pino, Pinuzzu, Peppe, etc, to distinguish the person. Each family's "Nina" became known as "Nina di Francesco" or Ninuzza, or some derivative. My cousin Rosalia became Rosalina, then Linuccia, then Ina. I became Florence, thanks to my Americanized sisters, but many years later, Flavia is considered a beautiful name. Maybe I'll ask to be re christened.

My generation tried to break away from tradition and we selected American sounding names. I have a son named Kenneth. There is no "K" in the Italian alphabet and the sound "th" was impossible for my mother to pronounce,so, he quickly was re named "Kenn ed ee" or "Ken nee."

Today Italian names are associated with glamour and are trendy so Fabio, Giorgio, Francesca, Gianni, Michela, Gabriela, Daniela, etc, have been used even by non Italian Americans.

I'm waiting for the day my father's name, "Melchiorre," becomes the name of the year, maybe in the next century. With Baldassare and Gaspare it is well known as one of the Three Wise Men. I just couldn't name any of my sons Melchior. They would never speak to me.

I do have a namesake though. My sons named their boat for me and "FLAVIA," in bold script, is written across the stern.

I guess I'll have to be satisfied with that, and, Kimberly and Sabrina are beautiful names for my two precious granddaughters.

SUNDAY CARS

What luxury I experienced when a white stretch limousine came to pick me up recently. It had seats for twelve people and was equipped with TV, air conditioning, tinted glass, bar, plush seats and it was so long you had to speak to the driver by phone. I was only going to the airport but thought *"If my parents could only see me now."*

We never owned a car. I remember when public transportation was the only choice and the elevated Culver line and West End, BMT lines were safe and quite dependable.

Very few families had cars when I was young. Business vehicles were the first priority for the new American citizens. My father had a big green Studebaker truck he used to carry produce from the market in Manhattan. My uncle had a 40's panel truck painted white to deliver eggs and cheese. The trucks were strictly utilitarian except for dire emergencies.

One morning I had a dilemma and my father was commissioned to drive me to school. I was humiliated to arrive in a big smelly truck with the calligraphy name on its doors I begged my father to drop me off a block away from the school. After all, I should have arrived in no less than a Cinderella chariot as far as my second grade students were concerned!

When businesses grew, the new entrepreneurs purchased "Sunday cars." Like Sunday clothes they were special, clean and quality.

Only a Cadillac, Chrysler or Packard was fit for Sunday afternoon rides for "La Signora," "Nonna," and the kids. With heavy chrome bumpers, plump white-walled tires and high gloss paint, these cars built status among the relatives.

I vaguely recall some small cars, sport coupes, with what I though was a large glove compartment on the exterior of the car just under the rear windshield. When opened the "rumble seat" was accessible by jumping on the running board, then one foot on the stepping plate in the rear fender and into the love seat for two, for a wind blown ride. They tell me those seats were also good for mothers-in law. Running boards made good seats for kids when the cars were parked at the curb. Sometimes the fenders were used as seats until the owner told you to get off. There were no alarms to frighten half the neighborhood.

What cars today compare with the old Chevy Bel-Aire, Nash, Packards or even a 1929 Buick Marquette? Certainly not my Camry!

Cars had character then. Although I developed an aversion to trucks from my childhood experiences (riding in the back of a truck and being jostled with no seat belt) I might be amenable to a ride in a Lexus or Mercedes Utility Vehicle—but a Hummer, Never! It has no esthetic qualities for me.

Mamma and the Sunday car in the 40s.

ROMAN BATHS

When I renovated my house I decided that one of my bathrooms should have a dramatic black jacuzzi bathtub, oversized shower, skylight and mirrored walls. That was hardly what I grew up with.

We had a small pink and blue tiled bathroom that was modern but there was only the one bathroom for six people. This didn't appear to present a problem until my wedding day.

In the commotion of preparations for an 11 o 'clock mass and photographer arriving for candid shots, my grandmother slipped into the bathroom before anyone else for the special day: "u sposaliziu di Flora"

"Nonna, I'm getting married. Let me in."

"Aspetta un minuto," she answered.

"Un minuto" was 12 precious minutes that I needed.

Nonna came out powdered, hair combed and ready for photos and I rushed my shower, makeup and left a clip in my hair for the entire day.

When I was a kid we would go to visit relatives in walk up apartments (tenement) in Greenwich Village. A tiny dim lit toilet was in the hall shared by other families and the bathtub was in the kitchen! I can still see it! The big vat lined up against the wall along side the sink and stove, with a porcelain cover that doubled as counter space. Water was heated when needed. If the lady of the house was into interior decorating she made a skirt for the tub to hide the legs or dark sides.

Could these newly arrived Americans ever foresee accessibility to steam showers, warmed towel racks, cushioned toilet seats, or whirlpool baths? But the Romans had that insight! Being a physically clean society, they built magnificent bath facilities. I recently visited the ruins of the Baths of Caracalla in Rome, which could accommodate three thousand people. In Pompeii I saw the steam room with it's curved ceiling that allowed collection of the warm condensed water in troughs. In Sicily I was amazed at the inventive hot water system at the Roman villa of Piazza Amerina. All were adorned with magnificent mosaics and hmm "...interesting" frescoes. These bath facilities all demonstrated Roman ingenuity. New York City also ran bath houses but I suppose not of the grand style of the Romans.

The immigrants survived under difficult conditions and even created a new word, "backhouso," which became a popular broken English word. I don't know what the plural of that would be for today's single family homes with three, four or more bathrooms.

Could the turn of the century immigrants ever foresee multiple bathrooms in single family homes?

What happened between the time of the Roman baths and the time of the immigrant. How did the grandeur that was Rome end up with a bath tub in the kitchen?

Granted I do not have frescoes in any of my three bathrooms but I insisted on Italian tiles on the floors and walls. All the amenities are confined to a bright and airy space but my children have been deprived of "Aspetta un minuto."

Caterina Castello Drago, Nonna.

ALL'APERTO

I learned theater etiquette at an early age.

"Please, please, let's go *all'Aperto!*" I would beg.

It was easy to convince my mother, grandmother and godmother that the very long walk to the open air theater was good for digestion. After the traditional Sunday meal of macaroni with meat sauce, a roast, vegetables, salad, fruit and pastries, surely a little exercise was required. My father stayed home to read "Il Progresso" and rest on his only day off.

The trio created a walking garden of blossoms with the patterns on the dark silk dresses they created on their old trusty "Singer." As they strolled, the body shapes accentuated by bosoms and buttocks, shifted the print of roses, or carnations on the fabric as a soft summer breeze off the Mediterranean Sea would sway poppies growing in a field in Sicily. They were a sight to behold as they walked in unison, with me in tow.

Still wearing the immigrant hairdo of a tight bun at the nape of the neck, they were fragranced by body talc, wore sensible black leather oxfords and carried pocketbooks that contained the family jewels. A ring, gold cross, or earrings from the old country were cherished as a remembrance of a sacrament day, as were a few photos of loved ones left behind.

My grandmother listened (as did most Italian immigrants) to a serial story on the radio every day. I learned to identify the opera arias that were the themes for the stories and products advertised.

The theater presented a sequel of the "romanzo" and gave the opportunity to match a body and face to the voice on the radio. Sometimes the girth of an actor was quite a surprise.

At dusk, the overture began and with no amplifiers, the violins and piano dominated the sound of the music. I would stare at the hand painted roll up curtain, with it's scene of a slightly spewing volcano, Italian pines, and hill of flowers, and dream of going there some day. We sat on folding wooden chairs that were set up in rows in the church yard of Most Precious Blood, a parish on Bay 50th St. in Brooklyn. The circus type tent with flaps on two sides shielded the audience from rain and wind and helped with the acoustics. A singer or comedian opened the show. Then the drama began. Yearning love, betrayal, deceit, tragedy, and romance were all presented on stage, in Italian! I was fascinated by the prompter's box when the words were so loud everyone knew the next line.

I awaited intermission so that I cold buy a special pizza of fried dough with a little sauce on it that I still savor today. I enjoyed watching the theater owner make it at the small outdoor kitchen that was really the concession. I also bought salted pumpkin seeds in little cellophane bags.

My introduction to live theater *all'Aperto* taught me to be a courteous member of the audience. I learned to respect and appreciate an actor's ability to express emotion and articulate beautiful language. I gained a love for live theater that continues today, but alas, the special snacks are not available on Broadway.

I DO I DO

I love weddings and feel honored when I receive an invitation. I enjoy seeing the glow of love on the young beautiful faces of the couple as they start a life together. After the months of anxious planning for the dream day, everything usually turns out well.

I'll never forget one church wedding I went to long ago. The church pews were decorated with flowers, the bride glowing and wearing the most expensive dress her family could afford walked down the aisle with her proud father. At the altar rail the father kissed the bride and gave her to the tuxedoed groom. The priest conducted the ceremony, the couple exchanged vows "for better, for worse" and then the groom was handcuffed and led away by the immigration police! He had entered the US illegally from Italy. He never attended the wedding reception. The bride left the church in tears and all the guests proceeded to the reception. It made headlines the next day.

Years ago Italian weddings were unique. Sandwiches wrapped in clear paper and pitchers of foaming beer and wine were the fare. At times particular sandwiches were switched and flung across to the next table thereby calling the affair a "football wedding."

I remember many children having fun sliding on the dance floor. I was one of them. The ethnic band sometimes on key sometimes not, kept the guests dancing mazurkas and tarantellas (or a Tango). A relative, who usually sang better than a professional, would entertain and white doves were let loose for good luck. Everyone waited for the cream puffs and cookies as the bride and groom distributed "confetti," sugar coated almonds with a silver spoon (later in a paper heart) and collected the gift envelopes (*la busta*). The cash filled envelopes were immediately relayed to the guardian in charge of the "busta bag". The large white satin, lace-trimmed, drawstring bag was traditionally homemade and the Nonna or an old aunt held it tightly in her lap and guarded it with her life. She was more secure than a Brinks truck! A few months ago my great nephew had a beautifully decorated box for the same purpose. I was "greatly" disappointed!

The Grand March was the signal that the party was over. With Rockettes precision the march began with a line, two then four then six abreast and more. Sometimes a long roll up group picture were taken of this finale.

During WWII when the groom was about to be shipped out, quick wedding celebrations were held at home with the family providing a banquet of homemade specialties.

Last summer, I went to a wedding on the beach! The bride wore ballet slippers and before wedding promises were made the couple chased each other in the sand. All the little nieces and nephews in bare feet followed the bride and waded in the sea. Candid photographs were taken with veil flowing and the groom passionately kissing the bride in a back- curving embrace.

My parents' 1922 wedding portrait looks like they were standing at attention. My mother's very young face looks lost in the oversized headpiece because it was borrowed at the last minute. Her original choice was stored under the bed and the family cat had shredded it and made holes in the netting. We still have an oval mirror with metal sepia photo affixed to it. They barely knew each other.

The marriage ceremony on the beach was celebrated by a Rabbi and a minister. During the joyous party we danced the Merenque, Samba and the Hora. We drank frozen daiquiris and margaritas and had a choice of entree- fish, chicken, beef, but all I wanted was capicolo on a soft roll wrapped in waxed paper and cream soda.

Years ago a personally delivered invitation meant you were a prestigious guest. Now some invitations tell you what to wear. I protest. I will not wear a black tie if I feel like wearing my red dress.

Somehow the vows lasted longer years ago. NOW divorce proceedings can start before the wedding thank-you notes go out. I wonder how many of these new marriages will celebrate their 50th?

SOME OLD PHOTOS

I assume everyone has a box of old photographs somewhere in the house. I was surprised to find some of mine in a battered suitcase in my basement. With curiosity, I glimpsed at a few of the faded rectangles and felt a flurry of emotions from sad to giddy.

"Is that young person with the small waist and big hair really me?"

I had to look twice. I laughed and relived the moments when I rode on an elephant in India, a camel in Morocco, and the best ride of all, in a red Alfa Romeo Spider in Italy with a movie star handsome Italian, my cousin! All were captured for perpetuity.

There were snapshots of people who were a big part of my life at one time and are gone now, friends, cousins, godparents, and others that I loved. They are being slowly forgotten, except for the proof that they existed - the photos. NOW those visuals create a rush from the annals of my memory.

What are we supposed to do with old photos? I think they test the resilience of the human spirit because your life flashes before you in speedy segments as you glance at them.You wonder where time has gone.

Through the silence of the photos I can still recall with vivacity the words that were uttered at that precise moment in time: "I do," "Auguri," "Happy birthday," "Addio," or even "formaggio!"

Pictures were important when grandparents and relatives were still in Italy years ago. We sent studio portraits of first communion and confirmation celebrations. They in turn sent occasional "ritratti" of the family overseas. A single black and white picture enclosed in a sporadic letter was usually of a large group shot in "campagna" (where there was sunlight and no need for a flash). I found one old sepia print with eight cousins posed around a 10-foot high "cisterna"! I remember my uncle's arid land depended on that water tank for irrigation. Everyone wanted to go to America, albeit by photo!

They say a picture is worth a thousand words. That is about how many I have said to my new digital camera. I have pleaded with my new "Digi', to do what I want, cajoled it, and said many sweet words to it, but it is still driving me crazy. I can send E-mail pictures NOW directly to Italy from my camera or cell phone. If only I can get my computer to cooperate.

I am from the era of the Brownie box camera, the awkward box with a viewer where the image was upside down. You had to load the camera with film for an eight or twelve image capacity, and remember to turn the film to avoid a double exposure. The costly developing service at the pharmacy took weeks. The black and white photos had a pinked border and colored film was a luxury.

Some of us can recall the classic newspaper images of a happy sailor kissing a nurse in Times Square in the 40's, John John saluting at JFK's funeral, or the smoldering Twin Towers on 9/11. We can feel those images penetrate into our hearts.

I cherish my photos with celebrities I've met over the years-then mayor of Rome, Giovanni Rutelli, Gore Vidal in Ravello, Lou Carnesecca at my Alma Mater, Matilda Cuomo, Billy Baldwin, Walter Wolfe.

Our family photos carry our personal stories. We want to savor the first birthday when fingers went into the cake. We want to remember Nonna's 90th birthday and hope to live that long. We want to remember our babies, little league games, recitals, our pets, milestones and holiday celebrations. We take pictures; then they become old photos!

I found my parents wedding portrait from 85 years ago and another of two WWI Italian soldiers, my father and my uncle. I could identify them because their names were on the back. Others, I wonder, "Who were they in my lineage?" They say a photo is a secret and the more it tells the less you know. "What were they like?" I can't throw these pictures away. They are a legacy! Maybe I can mount these heirlooms on a wall and let them become conversation pieces.

So NOW I have a lifetime of photos to sort out. I try to sequence them in preparation for an electronic archive for posterity, but I become overwhelmed. I stop, and become haunted by the images of long ago. They draw me back. I start again. Sometimes I wish it were THEN.

BREAKFAST, LUNCH, AND SUPPER

Growing up in an immigrant home, our eating habits were, unusual, old world, continental, hearty, healthy, delicious, Italian!

Breakfast for me was black espresso coffee with milk and biscotti. No, there were no Starbucks then but anise biscuits, angeletti, salivati biscotti, or regina cookies with sesame seeds were available from the local bakery or even home baked. Those were my daily choices before I went to school when I was a kid. It was an unusual start of the day for a young student because coffee was supposed to stunt your growth and cereal had all the nutrients in it to give you energy. I had my grandmother's Sicilian hometown breakfast menu and I survived. Nonna warmed up the coffee in a small sauce pan and added milk and sugar to it. It sounds like today's capuccino to me. We did not have a machine. The biscuits were perfect for dunking. My friends had oatmeal or soggy cornflakes.

I sometimes had olive oil sandwiches for lunch. Olive oil is a staple in Italian homes. We usually had a five gallon unmarked tin in our kitchen as well as some bottles of thick green home made oil sent to us from "il paese." Today it is called virgin olive oil or premium grade and we used it only to season our salads or vegetables. When the bakery across the street lured us with the intoxicating smell of bread being taken out of the oven I knew what my lunch would be. I brought the piping hot loaf of plain or seeded Italian bread home, wrapped in white paper. My mother would slice it length-wise and drizzle the oil on it. With a little black pepper, maybe an anchovy, and cut into quarters it made for a cholesterol free lunch. Delicious.

We had pasta for dinner every night, with vegetables, soup or *asciutta* with fresh tomatoes marinara. We ate fish to adhere to meatless fridays, small servings of meat on some other days, and because my father had a produce store, always vegetables. We ate well. When Jell-O and Twinkies were becoming popular we continued the Italian custom of having fruit for dessert. Pastries and soda were reserved for Sundays and holidays. We ended our meal with a piece of cheese and fruit. Usually the head of the family peeled an apple, a pear or an orange, sliced it and offered everyone a piece. Sometimes we had what I called "funny fruit," prickly pears, persimmons, figs, pomegranates and blood oranges native of Sicily. The tinge of red throughout the fruit also made a deep colored fragrant juice. We heard

38

the stories about the exquisite fruit of Italy. The lemons were huge. The tangerines were sweeter than sugar and grapes were as big as plums! The immigrants of long ago yearned for the favorite fruits from their towns and they tried to grow them. Almost everyone in the neighborhood had a fig tree. We had a mulberry tree in our back-yard that bore both sweet white berries and dark purplish berries on different branches. My father used grafting skills he learned as a boy in Sicily to accomplish this enigma. We would shake the branches and collect the berries in a sheet. In Italy, mulberry trees nourish silkworms that spin silk threads for fabric. Some of these exotic fruits are native to Asia and perhaps Marco Polo introduced them to Italy along with pasta! I remember special peaches soaked in wine and huge cherries soaked in pure alcohol. Sometimes we ate fresh al-monds that came encased in their green pod, chestnuts, or carobs. I always heard of "cotugna," (quince) a pear like fruit and "nespola" (loquat or medlar, a highly perishable apricot look alike with a large pit), but never tasted them until I went to Italy. They do not grow in the cold climate of New York but are sometimes available in gour-met green grocers today. Funny fruits were a delicious and healthy dessert.

RAP AND RHYMES BY NONNA

"A my name is Anna and my husband's name is Albert. We come from Alabama and we sell -apples." That was our RAP years ago. All this was a sing song rhythm to a bouncing ball on the sidewalks of New York and our creative recreation years ago. You bounced a ball until you missed it and the next kid started. The names used were revealing about your secret love and your food preference There were no sexual innuendos but sometimes youthful humor and childish themes came through like," Gina and Gerard coming from Greece selling girdles!"

Although Rap and Hip Hop are so popular now the words and messages are baffling to me. I have studied languages and my ear is trained to pick up a few words to make sense of spoken sentences but I confess I do not understand anything in the Rap/Hip Hop song world. There is no sweet or soothing melody, only rhythm and certainly no rhythm that I enjoy. Themes and vocabulary can be controversial.

Sometimes the rhythms remind me of my grandmother's ditties carried from Sicily in her mental computer. I think she was the origin Rapper!

Nonna taught me many of these rhymes, we might call limericks today, because I spoke Sicilian before I spoke English. I was precocious and often had to recite these little stories on demand. They were a bit risqué but I did not know it . Many had reference to bodily functions and were downright funny. Nonna had the rhythm and never missed a beat. I remember she laughed at herself when she taught me these:

Una volta c'era unu	There once was a man
Mangiava pani e pruna	Eating bread and prunes
Cull'ossu s'affucò	He choked on the pit
e tutt'i causi si cacò!	And in his pants he shit

Ring Round Rosie, Nonna's Sicilian version was so old it made reference to the King of Italy. I had to be animated for this one and flopped on the floor on cue.

Domani è domenica	Tomorrow is sunday
Ci tagliamo la testa Menico	Off with Menico's head
Menico non c'è.	Menico is away

Ci tagliamo la testa al Re	We will behead the king
Il Re è malato	The King is ill
Ci tagliamo la testa al soldato	We will behead the soldier
Il soldato è alla guerra	The soldier is at war
e vai dar il culo a terra	Oh, go flop on the floor!

A friend told me this one, obviously to help a young child toilet train

L'uccellino volò, volò	A little bird flew and flew
Sopra un albero si posò	Alighted on a tree
Posando disse	When he landed he said ,
Pe pe, pe pe, pe pe	Pee pee

Perhaps if Italian kids played the bouncing ball game, they would sing "C my name is Caterina and my husband's name is Calogero, "We come from Catania and we sell castange!"

It would be a shorter game skipping J, K,W X, and Y that do not exist in the Italian alphabet. At the named letter your leg had to turn over the ball with ease or you were OUT!

Nonna's fierce rhymes, verses and colorful vocabulary never touched on Mama, who was sacrosanct. Mama was the protector and was portrayed in this ditty.

Ma Ciccio, mi tocca	Ma Frankie is touching me
Ciccio non toccare la picciotta	Frankie don't touch the young lady
Toccami Ciccio, toccami	Touch me Frankie , touch me

That little dialogue with whinny inflections was a coquettish mini drama followed by giggles.

Nonsense rhymes entertained the older generation and children as oral tradition.

Nasca padasca	Nosey posey
Parente della musca	The flies friend
Viene la musca	Along comes a fly
E caca la nasca	And the nose sneezes

Oh yes, the old folks had the embryo conception of Rap in their minds. It was poetry, spontaneous, ad lib, creative, and silly humor. Hopefully some of these folklore gems will be preserved.

I do, I do, October 29, 1922.

The Neighborhood

The Neighborhoods in America section reflects how Italian Americans altered the area they lived in. Their needs and traditions became visible in gardens, stores, and everyday life. While a new allegiance was being formed, the surroundings maintained a flavor of Italy. The experiences recorded are real and spiked with humor.

Get the olive oil!
Babbaluci in a
Palermo Market.

Are these mushrooms safe?

44

"WHAT'S A STOOP?"

How does one explain the phenomena of "a stoop" to suburban bred "yuppies"? Officially it was the outdoor brick or cement stairway up to your house in the old neighborhoods of the city, but in reality a stoop created a lifestyle.

If you were lucky enough to have a stoop, it was a place to share secrets as a teenager, a place to sew in the sunlight for your grandmother, a place to smoke a pipe for your grandfather and of course the requirement to play stoop ball, for the kids on the block.

Playing stoop ball had particular rules. You caught the ball on one bounce or you were out. If you were skilled, the ball hit the tip of a step, you caught it on a fly and doubled your points. A pink Spaulding ball and stoop made you the most popular kid in the neighborhood.

On hot summer nights, after work and supper, older folks, used the stoop as an extension of their living rooms. With no air conditioning or cable TV, neighbors sat on the steps until the wee hours solving the problems of the world, chatting, even gossiping! I can still hear the banter.

"The Dodgers are gonnna win the pennant, not the Giants."

"Jackie Robinson's the best!"

" What? Are you kidding? Joe Di Maggio's gonna bring the Yankees to the World Series, you'll see!"

Upstairs and downstairs neighbors, sometimes engaged in arguments as hot as the temperature but the war could be shattered by the jingle of the ice-cream truck. "Good Humor, any one?"

We always played near the stoop. We used the fifteen cent Spaulding to hit a popsicle stick or penny placed on a line between two boxes on the sidewalk. We took turns and counted points to determine the winner.

If you were able to "borrow" a piece of chalk from school, the afternoon activity was set for potsie or hopscotch. A piece of white plaster retrieved from "the lots" sometimes worked just as well to chalk up the nine box grid.

As we prayed "Please no rain so we can play again tomorrow!" Mr. LoBianco would yell, "Don't write, in front of my stoop!"

The stanchions on the sides of the stairs were the most coveted seats and comfortable ones unless planters were cemented to them .

Ornate wrought iron railings also eroded the choice seating. City stoops sometimes framed small gardens with a statue, always roses and perhaps a shade tree.

Rather than standing on the corner watching all the girls or boys go by, we sat on the stoop watching all the world go by. Those were the days of dreaming, wishing, planning for the future, falling in love with the delivery boy and hoping for your first kiss, (on the stoop.)

Sunday in front of the stoop.

CYCLONE, TORNADO AND THUNDERBOLT

There is no doubt, Disneyland is special, a fantasy land exciting, entertaining, expensive, but to me it's still a glorified amusement park. I don't feel deprived that there were no theme parks when I was growing up. I experienced the prototype for all amusement parks-CONEY ISLAND!

As a teenager my free summer recreation was going to the beach. A few girls would take the elevated train or trolley to the last stop and walk over to Bay 14 or Bay 7 depending on which boys you hoped to see that day. We brought lunch, a cutlet or potatoes and eggs for me on Italian bread (that became a bit soggy, but delicious despite a few grains of sand in it) while my friends bologna with mustard turned grey by the time they ate their sandwich.

At about three o'clock we headed home for a shower and to tend to the sunburn, but not before indulging in a ride on the Cyclone. A quarter for the thrill of the Cyclone was worth it. With damp bathing suits and sand digging into our skin, we competed to get into the first or last car to feel the wind more intensely. I can still remember the slow ascent of the first hill and the quick second, steeper, slightly curved drop that lifted you out of your seat. We were not always loyal and tried the Tornado and Thunderbolt which were faster and literally made your hair stand up. They are gone but the Cyclone still runs today and has maintained its sensational reputation.

We couldn't pass up the scooters because the barkers called us in. These bumper cars hit hard enough to cause whip lash. The electrified cars sparked and we purposely got tangled in crashes to need the help of the cute guys who worked there.

We dared each other to try the parachute jump. Of course, we didn't jump free fall. It was a long slow way up the steel frame, a slight bump at the top and a fast way down to retrieve your shoes that had fallen off as you ascended. You felt as though you were at the top of the world with view of the sea and, if you dared to turn around, most of Brooklyn. It was spectacular and worth the fearful ride, but just once.

The parachute had been part of the 1939 World's Fair. Today it has landmark status, and the light at the top helps guide ships into the harbor.

Although every town has carnivals and temporary Ferris wheels, Coney Island has the most famous of all: The Wonder Wheel. It is huge! Most people would get into the gondolas thinking it would be a calm scenic ride but soon would find out that the swinging cars slid down a track with such force and noise that you were sure you would end up in the Atlantic Ocean. The Wonder Wheel still operates but I think I 'll skip it; the memory is still vivid.

The Steeplechase sign, a man with a big smile, lots of teeth and hair parted in middle, lured you in there through the gigantic turning barrel so that you could race on the Steeplechase horses. The sound was distinctive and you heard it from the beach.

Who knows how safe these rides were but we were young, daring, indestructible, and laughed all the way home, but not before we got dizzy on the carousel. The calliope music drew us to the ornate horses and we tried to catch the gold ring to get a free ride.

Sometimes I think the roller coaster rides were foreshadowing for my life. Up and down, curves and sharp turns but hopefully I end up laughing. Would I go on the Cyclone again? Maybe on a dare or a very large wager. Been there, done that!

THE CANDY STORES

When I was in elementary school, my world was restricted to a few blocks near my house. The neighborhood was dotted with vacant lots and I was allowed to go on errands to the "corner grocery store, to the bakery, or to the drug store. I could cross the avenue only to go the biggest building in the world to me, the five story PS 216.

Luckily, within my limited parameter was the candy store. It was strategically located across the street from the school and it was a fantasy land to me. Most of the kids went home for lunch and on the way back to school we made a quick stop at the "canny store." There, the glass shelves and high counter displayed enough candy to create instant cavities or a sugar rush to drive the teachers crazy for the rest of the afternoon.

For a penny you could get two twists of licorice, unwrapped, handed to you by Mr. G, a chubby old man whose glasses were as thick as his accent. For one cent you could get Mary Janes (peanut butter filled taffy) that stuck to your teeth, or small Hershey or Nestle chocolate bars. There were Baby Ruths, chocolate-covered marshmallow twists, or Butterfingers, You could buy little bottles of wax, filled with colored sugar water, pastel colored dots on a strip of paper, that were easy to share, cinnamon hearts, or sugar cigarettes in a little box, if you wanted to pretend to be a glamorous movie star. There were novelties like candy necklaces, red wax lips for two cents, Tootsie rolls, and root beer flavored lollypops.

We abandoned Juicy Fruit and Dentine gum for the new Bazooka bubble gum. With its distinctive scent and flavor we made bubbles as big as our faces all the way back to school, and then stuck it under·the desk when the teacher detected it. Chewing gum in school was a mortal sin!

In the Spring. a square glass case appeared on the counter. It displayed and protected the delectable Charlotte Russe from fingers that could spoil the whipped cream swirl on top. The pinked cardboard collar held a strip of sponge cake and ultimate indulgence cream. When the word spread that the candy store had Charlotte Russe, we bartered good behavior and begged for the extra few cents from our mothers to experience the delicious confection.

Although this candy store did not scoop ice cream, it did have Melo-rolls! The cylindric ice cream came with a perforated paper wrapper that was peeled off as it was placed sideways into a wafer holder and was tantalizing. I would pay at least a dollar for one right NOW, but I think they cost under ten cents THEN.

My Sunday routine was to go to a different candy store. I stood at the entrance and the proprietor gave me our reserved copy of Il Progresso and The News, and one bottle of cream soda. I did not even have to ask. I just stood there, gave the man the exact change, pivoted and ran home.

On the next block in my Italian American neighborhood, there was another candy store but it was off limits for me. My parents warned me not to go there because it was a hangout for some kind of "books." I liked books and could not understand why I could not go to Mr. Di's to buy my favorite comic book, Little Lulu. I went there a few times with my older sister to buy her favorite magazines, Photoplay and Modern Screen. I had to promise to hold her hand the whole time we were there. That candy store also made a special fountain drink, Egg Creams. They did not have an egg in them; just seltzer, chocolate syrup and a bit of milk, and it made the best carbonated refreshment.

In the morning people stopped at the candy stores to buy newspapers to read on the subway. In the downtown areas there were "adult" candy stores like Baraccini's, Bartons and Loft's. Valentine's Day was the busiest day for those chocolatiers. Gentlemen brought their sweethearts beautiful red hearts filled with chocolate assortments.

NOW, while I enjoy Perugina Baci and Ghirardelli bonbons, I keep thinking about the little cardboard box of pink, purple, yellow, blue or white sugar hearts from the candy store years ago that said KISS ME, BE MINE, I LOVE YOU. I would be so happy if I found one that said

"AMORE MIO!"

BOCCE

Empty lots in the neighborhood were our playgrounds when I was growing up. Parks were in the planning stages before the building boom of the post war years, so we made our own fun zones in the vacant land near our homes. Some kids made a clearing for a sandlot and played stick ball after school. The stick was an authentic cut off broom "stick." Lacking a stick we played punch ball and ran bases anyway. At night we played "kick the can" under a corner street light and used the sewer grid and manhole covers as designated bases. We improvised and it did not matter if the base lines were equidistant.

Adults played in the lots too! The old men in the neighborhood competed with the kids for lot space so that they could play bocce!

There was an old man, a distant relative, who was very enterprising. He created a bocce court in a large lot in the neighborhood. He did not own the land; he just took squatters' rights, probably from the city. He was known as the Bocce Boss because he owned the bocce sets and charged the players twenty-five cents per game. He commissioned his grandsons to carry the heavy wooden balls out of the garage and to the lot every day. There were at least three games going on at any given time. Retired men, those who worked night shifts or had the day off gathered in the "bocce lot" on a regular basis. It was their hangout, their piazza substitute. Wives knew where to send a runner with a message if necessary. As the men waited for their turn to play, they sat under the shade trees on the periphery of the courts. They would discuss the problems of the world and perhaps also enjoy a little "homemade refreshment."

Italians play bocce, French play boules, English play lawn bowls-all variations of a game that was amusement for Roman soldiers. They tossed small stones toward a larger stone and then progressed to rolling balls.

The aim of the game is for players to throw or roll the larger balls to get as close as possible to the target ball, the "pallina." Two teams vie for twelve points and the four balls for each team are color coded. Each player throws or uses a crouch strategy to roll the bocce to get inside the other players space. The opponents concentrate for precise aim. Players sometimes think they can coax the ball along by body language so the leg goes up, shoulders twist, or the face contorts, in anticipation. But the ball will go where it is destined anyway. The closer the balls the greater possibility for a point.

Then the fun begins. Determining the positions of the balls is serious business. If a visual estimate is doubted, a heated argument can ensue. Out comes the string, the perfect improvised measuring instrument, but accuracy again can be questionable! It can create havoc when hats and hands go flying! In lieu of a standard ruler, a player sometimes used to draw lines on an ordinary stick for an "accurate measure." that was also slightly off! NOW, they probably could install a computer chip in the bocce ball that says "closest to pallina," or "punto" in an animated computer voice that would solve the disputing.

I like to watch the men play bocce when I am in Italy. On my recent trip I saw a bocce pavilion in Spoleto. There were young and older gentlemen playing on indoor alleys set up side by side like bowling alleys. I wonder why I never see women playing bocce in Italy. I know both men and women enjoy playing at our picnics. Bocce is so popular in Florida that there are tournaments in the condo complexes. Warm breezes with palm trees swaying provide a soothing atmosphere, but still I see a toss up of caps and stomping to prove a point! I guess it is part of the game. Bocce is an enjoyable part of our heritage and ready for world recognition. It should be an Olympics sports event!

Bocce in Spoleto!

I WAS AN ANGEL

I was an angel a long time ago. I was not from a past life or the "Touched by an Angel" variety that can dissipate like an expiring rainbow, BUT a human, flesh and blood angel with wings and a halo. My "supernatural" life was on this planet, in this country, in New York state, in Brooklyn as I floated down the aisles of our Lady of Grace Church in holy day processions.

After First Holy Communion at about age seven, girls were allowed to join the angel sodality and boys joined the St Aloysius group (I never heard of anyone named Aloysius). THEN we were obliged to take part in every procession, and there were many of them. Parishes where Italian immigrants settled continued their old world devotion to their town patron saints. Celebrating your name day or saint's feast day was a special occasion and it usually meant a leisurely walk around the church, "a procession!" Southern Italians always had a special love for Santa Rosalia, St.Anthony, St.Lucy (no bread on Dec. 13), St Joseph and St Francis of Assisi. San Nicola had his following and San Gennaro made New York City's Mott Street famous.

I loved to wear the angel harness of white wings trimmed with gold and of course I felt absolutely divine wearing the sparkling halo. Hypnotized by the organ music and choir singing Panis Angelicus or Ave Maria, and walking slowly with hands in prayer position became a spiritual experience. The smoke and pungency of the benediction incense became ethereal and is memorable to this day.

Once a year the saints were taken for a walk. Actually their statues were carried on men's shoulders in procession around the neighborhood. A small band of off key musicians or a loudspeaker attached to the roof of a car blasting religious music announced the coming of the statue. People ran out of their homes to pin the money on the satin ribbons attached to the saint. People said a short prayer and for a moment Italy was in Brooklyn and the donation helped save your soul. Some devout members of the third order of St Francis even wore the brown St Anthony robes and walked barefoot in thanks for a special petition. These were not parades but a display of religious faith, and angels led the flock. Only girls were angels in those days and I was an angel. As a teenager I graduated to the St Teresa Sodality. We wore short brown and gold capes that were reversible for different occasions and a matching skull cap since female heads had to be covered in church at that time. We still participated in the procession but were farther down the line because we were taller.. We sang the Latin hymns we had learned by rote and recognized a few words from the Italian we spoke at home.

Later as young adult women you were allowed to join the Virgin Mary Society. The day that you married, you could wear a blue cape over your gown . The priest gave you a statue of the Madonna at the altar to keep in your home. After marriage ladies joined the Rosary society. Is this ancient history?

I looked forward to the pageants and processions. These were our recreational activities.

I think being in church groups started my fascination with angels. I love angels and always fly angels back with me (on the plane) when I return from Italy. I've bought gold leaf wooden angels in the catacombs in Rome, bisque angels in Florence for my Christmas tree and also small paintings of Raffaello's good and naughty angels in Urbino, Raffaello's birthplace.

Angels are sacrosanct and popular now. Many people wear angel pins and belief in the power of angels crosses religious lines. Italy's museums are filled with paintings and statues of cherubim and seraphim! Italian Angelos and Angelas are everywhere!

Church rituals have become somewhat generic now. My children were never in a procession and confirmation was in a unisex red robe for everyone.

I think I've had a guardian angel for many years. I'd like to be an angel again but I'll wait until I'm called. I've had practice, so I hope they let me into heaven even if my halo is a bit askew.

BABBALUCI!

Every May I plant an herb garden; parsley, mint, rosemary, basil, all grow well in my backyard. With my loving care, strong sunshine and occasional watering, so do the weeds!

Recently while weeding, I was greeted by a familiar pest, a slug, with a shell: a BABBALUCI! My weed pail had been left out in the rain and two more had taken refuge in the weed and water soup. These three were probably the culprits that made the holes in my basil leaves and my plum tomatoes.

Just then, a scene flashed before me of the many Sunday afternoons my family sat around an outdoor table eating snails that were steamed in garlic and oil or with a little bit of fresh tomato sauce.

I used to eat them! I looked at the creatures again, their striped spiral shells and little antler eyes were tempting me to keep them as pets or at least show them to my neighbors' children.

When I was a kid in Brooklyn, my father sometimes sold snails in his store. They came imported from Italy in a wicker basket and were usually "asleep" with a white membrane over the opening. I was intrigued by them and often touched them to see if they would retreat into their brown and white shells. Once, I left the cover off the basket and overnight they escaped and were stuck all over the walls of my father's store. He was not happy about that.

We would eat hundreds of them as an evening snack but it was really a recreational activity, "un passatempo."

Family and "paesani" chatted and laughed while we picked the snails out of their shells and remarked at the taste, the size, or the struggle to pull them out of their portable homes. Sometimes we were lucky to get the tiny ones, "babbaluceddi," which provided an added challenge to see who ate the most. Rather than a toothpick, a small pin was used to pull these little guys out. It was simple, family fun.

We also ate "tuppideddi," a more meaty type of snail or "lumache," a sea snail. That was then. Now an appetizer of eight escargot, on a sculptured plate, at a French restaurant costs twenty two dollars! You do get a clamp and special fork as tools to help you eat them though.

Eating snails, on the "terrazza," accompanied by homemade wine and crusty bread, followed by espresso and pignoli cookies are a fond memory of my childhood. It may sound like a scene from a movie but it was a scene at my house when I was growing up.

BIKES AND SKATES

Part of my exercise routine is a two mile walk at a park that overlooks the Great South Bay. I follow the shoreline while the burning sunsets that turn the sky to a blend of pink, blue and lavender entertain me. Seagulls, terns and small boats dart around in the rippling water. "Che bello!"

I share the blacktop path with baby strollers, bikers and skaters, a few fishermen and gaggles of honking Canadian geese

Oh, how I yearned for a "two wheeler" when I was a kid! Schwinn, pink, girls style, maybe streamers on the handle bars and of course a bell. My mother's veto power denied me that dream because a neighbor had been hit by a car in the street. That was it. No bike for me, forever!

So I substituted skating for my street activity. I could race, skate backwards, make sharp turns, and was almost an acrobat on my ball bearing skates.

I get unnerved sometimes when skaters approach me in the park and I haven't heard anything until I feel and hear the "Whoosh" of the wind as they pass me. I question my sanity and sense of sound at that point!

Where is the unmistakable sound of small metal wheels on cement of my days? The friction of those wheels on the pavement was heard from a block away and it usually meant.

"Get out of the way, I can't stop," as a of bunch of kids came bounding down the block.

The silent Roller blades have a row of four small plastic wheels and shoes! We had to attach our skates to our own shoes and fasten the small grips to the leather sole of our shoes so tightly that the sole would practically rip off. We wore the "treasured" skate keys around our necks on a string for the many times the skates fell off and had to be reattached. Later large felt lined safety clamps were invented that went over the front of the shoe. We still used the key but the skate stayed on longer.

I remember the distinctive sound of my metal wheeled skates and the rhythm created going over the sidewalk lines. That undeniable skate sound changed according to the pavement composition. We knew who had a new smooth sidewalk and where there was a sloping driveway to give us an improvised ramp. Today's skateboarders think they invented jumping ramps and platforms. We had them too! We did not wear helmets or knee pads and had plenty of scraped elbows!

We also had shoe skates but those were wooden wheeled and for indoor use at a rink. There, girls were allowed to wear very short skirts(reversible) and we skated in pairs and trios to organ music. As a young adult I learned to ice skate and the highlight of that sport for me was skating in the rink at Rockefeller Centre under the statue of Atlas holding up the world.

Old skates were never discarded. They were used to make scooters. The skate was taken apart. Two wheels were put on either end of a short beam. Then a crate was attached, upright, at one end and "PRESTO" you had a scooter! Two sticks made steering handles and bottle caps decorated the ingenuous contraption. The scooting sound also rivaled silence in the neighborhood.

Not motorized and not patented, scooters provided many hours of fun for the local boys.

Time and size have made me little off balance on skates NOW. I am past the scooter stage but maybe someday I'll finally get a senior citizen big wheeled tricycle!

THE CUSTOMERS

I was raised to believe that "the customer is always right." That was the motto for the Mom and Pop businesses in my neighborhood a long time ago. The storeowners, mostly immigrants, had an innate sense that all patrons were to be treated with respect- so that they would come back.

The customers in my parent's store, of course, were anonymous but with true Italian creativity we gave them identifying names. And what names they were!

Some of the unsuspecting clients had names such as "Corto Corto" or "shorty," only because of the gene pool that this very short man inherited, and another "Senza Denti," because his front teeth were missing. No one had a dental plan and dentists were expensive. "La Bionda" was simply "Blondie," due to her hair color and "Occhi Storti" was the crossed eyed lady with thick glasses.

Another customer was "Mosca sul Naso" because this woman had a dark wart on her nose that tempted you to swat it!

"Tacco Tiso" or (*Tacco Alto*) was a small lady who wore high heels all the time to look glamorous. My mother, in her oxfords, sometimes comically imitated the woman's saunter. "Faccia Tagliata" unfortunately had a scar on her face acquired as a child in Italy. There were no plastic surgeons available, so forever more, there was a disfiguring mark on her cheek.

"Meatballs" was a collective name for a large family who lived in a storefront, modified to be a residence. The father rarely worked and the grandmother supplied meatballs very often for dinner. Hence the moniker "meatballs" for any person in that family!

The names were not meant to be derogatory, in those days before political correctness sensitivity, but served merely to identify the people that came across the threshold of my father's store.

"La Signora" was a gentleman who proclaimed himself "the lady," because he switched gender roles at home. His wife worked, so he did the daily chores of shopping and cooking while home recovering from surgery. "La Fat" was an over weight woman whose real name was Giuseppina. While addressing her, we called her "Signora Josie" and stared at her belly. Although at times we reduced the price of late afternoon produce for her large family, her son is now CEO of a multi-million dollar corporation: a success story!

We had a "Secco, Secco," a slim, young, man who was a vegetarian and balked when some vegetables were treated with wax to enhance their appearance. He engaged my father to look for what we now call "organic" fruits and vegetables for him at the market. He was a good customer and ahead of his time.

We referred to people by their professions as well. "Il Professore" taught biology at St. John's University and influenced my choice for college. "Dottore" became our family physician and sometimes gave advice as he selected tomatoes. "Lo Scrittore" worked for Irving Berlin and brought me sheet music and "Il Sarto" was a tailor.

Sometimes we knew a person by their pets. Mrs. D'Agostino had "Regina" a little black and white dog that barked in Italian. But there was also a family we called "Cagnioli," "little dogs," because they were always fighting among themselves.

Of course, we used province names to refer to some customers too. So we had the "Gemelli Calabresi," tall lanky twins from Calabria. They reminded me of Smith Brothers cough drops because of their dark hair and goatees. A lady from Bari, we dubbed, "Sha Mu Neim," the "Let's go!" customer, because she was always in a hurry.

All in all these were colorful names for honest, faithful, customers, with no disrespect intended but maybe a bit of whimsy.

I do not know the derivation of the names "Funzy" or "Chickie," teenagers who lived in the area, but when their mothers came to the store, we labeled them, "Funzy" or "Chickie's mother".

We had a fascination with using funny descriptive nicknames and NOW, I wonder what the customers called the shopkeepers?

"DANCING IN THE DARK"

That was a romantic song of another era. In those days your dancing partner held you close, perhaps even "Cheek to Cheek" as another song suggested, and the music was smooth. We admired Ginger Rogers and Fred Astaire as the epitome of elegance as they floated across the movie screens.

There is a resurgence of ballroom dancing NOW and television programs make it a competition among celebrities. It is captivating to watch as couples glide and whirl about. The women half naked in spiked heels move gracefully to an orchestration of melodic music.

It was so different in my day when American Bandstand with Dick Clark was on TV. THEN, a bunch of teenagers jumped around and waved at the camera for all to see on a small black and white RCA at home.

My memory of learning how to dance goes back to lunchtime lessons in my school gym, with the lights on! I wore penny loafers and a pleated skirt. In warm weather we went into the school court-yard to the sunlight. The dance sessions were an alternative to fight-ing in the school cafeteria! A teacher volunteered to keep us busy with "social dancing". So we counted for the basic box step, one, two, three, four, and up to three for a cha-cha-cha, always hoping a Lindy would be next

All the effort was in preparation for confraternity dances and the Spring Hop. It was to no avail because usually the boys sat on one side and the girls on the other side in the church basement. It was an awkward age, so after the standoff some girls might dance together. There were also restrictions. If you danced the fox trot with a guy, you could not be too close. There was no dipping and you could not dance "The Fish" because it was deemed too provocative. The safe dances were the Bunny Hop and the Hokey Pokey. THEN came Elvis and everything changed. Everyone was rocking around the clock and doing a Shake, Rattle, and Roll. Later, we all caught John Travolta's Saturday Night Fever and the Disco clubs became alive at 11 P.M.

Folk dancing was part of the physical education program in my school. We learned the Virginia Reel and the Mexican Hat dance, but not the Tarantella. I wish we had learned the traditional Italian dance too. NOW when they play the familiar music at weddings

60

and affairs everyone likes to participate, but it seems that only a few people know how to do the dance correctly. We go around in circles, switch partners, and I usually go in the wrong direction. They say the origin of the dance was in the town of Taranto when someone in the nearby fields was bitten by a tarantula. Frenetic dancing was supposed to purge the poison from the body. So the person jumped, spun, and gyrated almost in a trance until they observed a supposed cure. Italians, being creative, added tambourine, mandolin, and guitar, and choreographed a dance. Most regions of Italy have a variation of the Tarantella but the best known are from Napoli, Calabria, or Sicilia .

Although I am envious of the grace and smooth body movements in ballroom dancing. I know I was never able to move like that. Just doing the Twist would knock my hip out of joint. Now I would rather do the Tarantella anytime. Take notice. Everyone smiles when they do our traditional dance. We should enjoy this part of our heritage and teach the circle dance at our meetings. We would have some lively clapping and stomping. After all the spider made us do it!

DRIVING SCHOOL

I just completed a driving course offered at my library for "seniors." I thought it was for "high school seniors" learning how to drive a car but then realized that "senior" might refer to me! My auto insurance company offers a 10% discount incentive so I decided to refresh my driving skills. Actually, I think I am a pretty good driver but my children might disagree. That's when I ask them "Who taught you how to drive?" I still remember my near coronary attacks as we practiced driving around the neighborhood when they had learner's permits. They considered stop signs optional and they insisted that the parked cars on the right were out too far from the curb. I remember shouting " We are not on the *autostrada* and you are not an Italian race car driver." When they accelerated my whole body lunged forward.

I took them out at night to train them to put the headlights on when they returned from their after school jobs. We practiced slow driving in the rain and U turns and parking in the school yard. On their 17th birthday at 7 A.M. we were first in line at the Motor Vehicles Bureau and the clerk greeted them with "Happy birthday and drive safely."

I felt as though I was the proprietor of "Flo's Driving School" when I had four teenagers eager to get access to wheels. They all learned to drive on the family station wagon. It was not a status car for them but for me in the late 70's the nine passengers light-blue Chevy Impala was like today's mini van for suburban families. We could car pool the whole Little League team. Seat belts were not mandatory. We carried a rowboat, crab nets and fishing poles with ease. My sons called it "the tank." I think they played bumper cars with it because it always came back with a scratch or little dents that "must have happened in the parking lot." I wish we had On Star then.

On homecoming day, my sons and their friends painted my car green, the school color. They posed the school football team on the roof, hood and fenders of the car. Then they photographed it for the school yearbook. I gasped when they drove the car home.

"Don't worry, Ma. We'll take it to the car wash. Give us the money."

We also discovered how far the car could go on fumes! I promised if I didn't make it to the corner gas station I would take away the keys for a month!

How different is was years ago. I did not get a driver's license until I was in my twenties. I learned to drive on a stick shift car that was not easy for me. Clutch- shift- brake, was too much for me to process. I remember practicing on the city streets and we used hand directional signals. The driver put the arm straight out for a left turn, bent at elbow for right turn and arm down for slow down. Only those signals and the horn were communication with other drivers. Windows had to be kept open on the driver's side. There were no air conditioning, no power brakes, no seat belts, and no car seats for children, in those days.

NOW my grandchildren have a battery operated Jeep and a Barbie convertible that they "drive" around their property at five and six years old. By the time it is legal for them to drive on a public street they will have enough experience to drive a red Ferrari.

I can't wait to go to Italy again. I feel qualified to drive a Maserati or a Lamborghini now. After all I passed the 55 Alive Defensive Driving course!

1982 Lancia Zagato, not a Maserati!

BLACKOUTS

New York has suffered great loss in recent months. Our famous "gemelli" collapsed before our very eyes and two months later an airplane fell out of the sky into a residential area. How could we ever prepare for this devastation? We have sophisticated surveillance methods now.

I have vague memories of sirens screeching, all lights out, shades drawn, and everyone remaining indoors when I was a youngster in Brooklyn. It was a "blackout" in the early 1940's during World War II. These were practice drills in case of enemy air invasions. Indeed a few Germans did come ashore along the Eastern seacoast. It is recorded that some landed on Long Island and also in Florida.

During the Civil Defense drill a warden with a white helmet, dressed in khaki, and an armband patrolled the block, blew his whistle, and through a megaphone ordered, "All lights out."

The warden was usually someone who did not qualify for the draft and was 4F perhaps because he had flat feet or was a bit older.

I was very young but I have a flashback of being huddled into our kitchen and my grandmother attempting to console us by making pizza, "sfingione" to be exact. What else do Italians do when they are anxious except make something good to eat!

The smell of herbs, tomatoes, anchovies and cheese could have lured the enemy right to our doorstep! Huge search lights flashed across the dark sky, the oven warmed us and we ate pizza by candlelight. This was my childish perspective.

My father fought for Italy in WWI and my brother fought against Italy in WWII. Despite the irony, Italian American families were patriotic and certainly maintained allegiance to the USA.

I remember some neighbors had small gold fringed banners hanging in their windows. Each star on the white satin was for a son in the armed forces Some women also volunteered-especially nurses and were called WACS or WAVES.

Many women worked in defense industries and were memorialized by Norman Rockwell as "Rosie the Riveter."

I hoped that I would never recall some of the details of those days but suddenly all of this is brought to mind and jumbled in my head. I remember the sirens on the train station being tested at noon, car headlights painted black, and lines at the grocery stores for coffee and sugar.

A few years ago when returning from a trip to India, my flight went over Afghanistan. The natural phenomena of the terrain and rugged mountains had everyone on the plane out of their seats peering out of the windows in amazement. Amid the harsh brown landscapes were isolated little villages. Kabul looked like a bigger village. No tall buildings, bridges or highways were visible, just earth tones created by sun and shadows-spectacular but ominous.

I think back now and say,

"How can anyone ever penetrate that territory to find the enemy?" I may have a solution. Perhaps the food drops should include some good pizza as "aroma warfare". We might be able to entice the bad guys out of those caves!

May our service men and women return safely and very soon.

POLIO SUMMER

I was under house arrest the summer I was nine years old. I didn't do anything wrong but there was a Polio epidemic in New York City at that time and no cure for the dreadful disease that could leave you crippled. The daily headlines gave an account of how many Polio cases were admitted to hospitals. Beaches were closed because of water pollution and we had to avoid crowds. Wearing camphor balls or garlic in a pouch around your neck was not going to ward off this dreadful illness.

My family was determined to protect me so I was isolated and spent most of the day on my personal "tar beach." Our kitchen door led to the "roof" area above a garage. It had a three-foot high brick wall enclosure and I was safe and quarantined! I was able to play ball and jump rope out there. I learned to play solitaire and if an adult had time we played checkers or Scoppa! I read an easy version of Luisa May Alcott's "Little Women" that summer.

We did not have a television yet but we had a phonograph and a few records by a new Italian American singer named Nicola Paone. I lip-synced his humorous songs through a paper megaphone to a captured audience, my grandmother and god parents. For my birthday my sister gave me a music album, Prokofiev's, "Peter and the Wolf." I memorized the themes and mimicked the movements of the animals and stomped around as the hunters. I played it so many times that I had to replace the phonograph needle so that the black 78's would not get scratched.

I learned to embroider and knit, but best of all I liked to use my imagination playing with paper dolls. My older sisters bought me Lana Turner and June Allison books that included elaborate, colorful costumes from the latest Hollywood movies. After I cut out all the clothes I used the tabs to dress the stiff paper dolls and with vivid imagination took all the parts in the little dramas that I created.

Late in the summer I went upstate with my cousins to their grandmother's farm in Highland. The disease was not as prevalent up there. We went to the Dutchess county fair where they judged the best of everything: cow, pig, pie and jam. I had a frightening experience when I went into a medical trailer. I saw a Polio patient in an iron lung (similar to an MRI tube)that did the breathing for her.

Only her head was exposed resting on a pillow. They needed donations for the child's continued therapy.

Our families witnessed the crippling effect of Poliomyelitis on President, Franklin Delano Roosevelt, who was wheelchair bound , and they feared the spread of the virus. In September when they gave us March of Dimes cards in school, we filled the coin slots and joined the campaign to find a cure.

I was spared from Polio, but I know people who were in charity convalescent homes for years. One of my friends remained with a thin leg and limped due to Polio. Not soon enough there was progress for a vaccine by Dr. Jonas Salk and they started an inoculation program. Then, in my first year of teaching I had to take the Sabin sugar cube oral vaccine along with my young students.

I was alone but not lonely with all the adults trying to keep me busy that hot summer. It was probably better than today's camp experiences. With a mind full of fantasy I was a conductor, an actress, various animals, Jo, Meg, Beth, Amy, and myself anxiously waiting to hit the double digit age of ten! NOW we worry about West Nile, Lyme Disease and SARS. Many of us can relate to the apprehension because we lived through that Polio Summer.

GARDEN LESSONS

"Why are you keeping dead flowers in the garage?" my son asked the other day. He used a tone that indicated my sanity was in question.

"I'm seed saving. I learned that from your Nonno. Seeds come from the flowers".

As far as my son was concerned all seeds came in little packets with pictures of flowers or vegetables on them and cost $1.59 at the garden center.

He was lucky I was only saving zinnias, and marigolds. I remember when my father kept a bulbous squash hanging on the fence for weeks until it began to look spooky. Later, it was harvested, cut open and the seeds were dried for the next planting season.

My father never bought seeds; he traded them with his customers. Each person bragged that the seeds came directly from *il paese* and were for the reddest tomatoes, biggest peppers and most fragrant *basilico*. These seeds changed hands as though they were diamonds wrapped in soft paper.

We started seedlings indoors, not in little biodegradable cells, but in anything that was available, including an old pasta pot. They were transplanted, placed in rows separated by wooden planks to walk on, just as they did in Italy.

I think my father was into organic farming because he used natural fertilizer. It was usually acquired from the last horse drawn wagon in the neighborhood. The wagon belonged to the "Junk Man" who unfortunately had lost an arm in the war. He wasn't able to drive a truck but he was able to direct his horse to our street where the horse regularly "plopped" a generous donation! My father would run out with a shovel to collect the manure and immediately place it around his plants. I stayed away from the garden on those days. Now I buy sterilized, odor free manure at the nursery.

The fertilizer worked especially well on the ugly, dark, and wrinkled roots my father called "patate." He stored them all winter in a paper bag in the cellar and planted them in early Spring. After a few weeks, tall stalks appeared from the ground.

My neighbor belongs to the local Dahlia Society. I know about dahlias! That's what the "patate" were, dahlia tubers! The magnificent flowers came in an array of colors and were so large and heavy they had to be staked up to support them. My father's Dahlia Society consisted of some old men on the block who compared their blooms across the counter in my father's store and sighed "che bellezza!" with emotional adoration for nature's beauty.

Although my father had a vegetable store, our crop was for personal use and there was always room for beautiful flowers. The Irises that grew along our fence became my favorite flower. I helped dig up and cut the rhizomes to give to our friends. We collected the beautiful purple stalks and filled our vases indoors, sometime we placed them at the outdoor grotto near our church. To this day, I have white Irises in my garden.

We had a rose bush in the middle of the yard that could rival any perfume, but whose purpose was to attract bees for pollination. We did not use pesticides, but particular flowers were planted to ward off insects. Weeding was done daily and if a dandelion dared sprout, the tender leaves were put into a salad that same day! If I see a little yellow flower, I buy weed killer the same day.

There were no swing sets in our yards then, we climbed trees. My favorite was our white berry tree. I remember the day some *paesani* helped my father cut off the branch that I used for balancing. They grafted another smaller branch onto the stump with surgical precision; the wound was sealed with a pasty nutrient mixture, bandaged and examined daily. By the end of the summer, we had a hybrid tree with white berries and black berries on different branches. It was the wonder of the neighborhood. The berries were larger and sweeter than before.

We had the traditional fig tree (that I was not allowed to climb) and a few peach pits thrown into the enriched ground became trees that produced a bounty of sweet peaches a few years later There was not an unproductive spot in the garden.

My children think I took a course in horticulture but I had a head start on gardening in Brooklyn, years ago.

The backyard was my playground where I observed, helped, and learned about planting the future from my father and godfather. I save seeds, trade cuttings and may plant dahlias *"patate"* this year. I know I inherited the Italian appreciation and respect for nature.

PRONTO!

I can be reached anywhere, anytime day or night by beeper, E-mail, FAX or cellular phone. I have so many numbers I can't memorize them all. If I'm not home my answer machine takes a message, or my voice mail picks up and then a little light alerts me that I'm wanted. Call waiting interrupts my conversation and call forwarding finds me anywhere. I can't hide!

I remember when very few people had telephones at home. My family had one because it was deemed a business necessity. We also had a standard black rotary model as an extension. Although not a conference call feature, it provided entertainment for some members of the family as they listened in.

I remember neighbors ringing our bell on Sundays pleading to use our phone for emergencies because the the corner candy store or drugstore was closed. There were no street phones and the distinctive dark brown phone booths were the only lifeline to doctors or relatives across town. The phone booth was about two feet square with embossed tin walls and a half glass bi-fold door. The wall design usually a "fleur-de-lis," gave your fingers something to trace during your conversation. The phone had three coin slots and was placed at an angle in the corner just awkwardly enough for a person to drop a nickel onto the floor of the booth. You then had to open the door to find it on the dark floor. The overhead light was invariably out of order and <u>perhaps</u> the little fan circulated when needed. You hit the jackpot with a free call if your nickel jingled down to the coin return. This was "high tech" in those days. Some booths had a corner shelf called "a seat" that you- sort of sat on. Somehow the telephone booth became an airless but certainly not soundproof cubicle. If you survived the ordeal of making a call under these conditions you probably didn't need to call a doctor anyway.

Telephone numbers had character years ago. We dialed letters of an exchange that hinted your location such as **CO**ney Island 5, **BE**nsonhurst 6, **E**splanade 6, **DE**wey, **CL**overdale, **MA**in, **MU**rray Hill, **EV**ergreen, **T**rafalgur, **In**gersol. Phone numbers became immortalized in songs and movies such as Glenn Miller's "Pennsylvania 6-5000," "Butterfield 8," "Dial M for Murder," and the thriller "Sorry Wrong Number." Very often radio commercials had their telephone numbers running through our heads. NOW with so many digits programmed for calls, I think I can get through to Mars!

The first time I went to Italy no one had a phone at home. I felt like "ET" trying to call home to tell my parents that I was OK. The SIP office (national telephone company) was not reliable and "gettoni" were heavy in your pocket. Even a call from one of the finest hotels on Via Veneto was a disaster. I was tempted many times to sing Nicola Paone's song "The Telephone No Ring.""No ringa, no ringa, no ring." Indeed, because there was no connection.

The last time I was in Italy it seemed everyone had a "telefonino" magnetized to an ear. I even saw a young man with a phone at each ear. Two girl friends? I took a picture of him!

I also saw a few people carrying on heated conversations with an invisible partner. Not so long ago that would have been cause for concern. An investigation into the imaginary friend would have been conducted by a psychiatrist. Once a little phone comes into view, all is well!

What a sight! The Coliseum background and millennium Romans on cellular! The ghost of Caesar must be in shock. If Julius only knew what the future had in store!

Do I hear a phone?

71

"GOING TO THE STORE"

Shopping in one of those MEGA stores is a nightmare! The carts are so big, giants could shop there ! The product sizes are designed for weight lifters and traipsing down the aisles could be a marathon. They sell everything from tires to pretzels, you can't find what you need and manage to spend $122 anyway! Where are the good old Mom and Pop stores?

Not so long ago (it seems), as the youngest in my family, my responsibility was to "go to the store" everyday after school. I lived in Brooklyn and food had to be FRESH.

I crossed the street to Cuccio's bakery - twice a day at the precise moment when the neighborhood was intoxicated with the smell of bread being taken out of the oven. A whole, just baked, bread was a requirement for lunch and supper. I went to the grocery store for cold cuts and sliced cheese. If they weren't just sliced I was instructed not to take them. I went to Giordano's pork store and watched them fill the casing with sausage meat right in front of me. I went to De Vito's Butcher shop and waited, with a view through the glass of the high refrigerated cases, while the butcher cut the veal cutlets my mother had ordered. I took the long walk to Mazzola's coffee store, in expectation of the aroma emanating from the coffee roasters. The shiny brass and copper tumblers turned hypnotically while some coffee beans were ground for my mother's "black coffee".

Chickens were so fresh, they were alive and clucking. A trip to the chicken market was like a visit to a mini zoo with rabbits and ducks and turkeys. The smell was awful. Friday was fish day, and it was caught, sold, and cooked on the same day.

My favorite errand was going to Savino's "Pastificio". I liked to watch the huge machines making the pasta under the direction of "Mr Jack." I remember the thick iron wheels with unusual holes in them that created the different shapes of pasta. It was truly a moving sculpture that miraculously created the mainstay of our diets from semolina wheat and water. Blades cutting and the noise of changing gears fascinated me. Long pasta, as we called linguine, spaghetti, or perciatelli, was then draped over wooden dowels and hung in a cavernous backroom. Pulleys raised and lowered the curtains of pasta until they were dry. We bought it as triple the length of today's boxed pasta and broke it in half ourselves at home. There were wooden bins labeled with whimsical names such as " ditali," "marruzelli," "cavatelli," " orecchini" where the maccheroni were stored. Soft pasta, fettuccine or margherita was available on certain days.

The only store I didn't visit was the fruit store because I lived upstairs. It was my parents' store . My mother was an active part of the business as were most of the women who worked beside their husbands. They became experts in customer relations and could give lessons to our MBAs. We ate a lot of vegetables. Sometimes my grandmother felt sorry for the remains of the day. "Peccato," she would say, and cleaned and created an edible medley of greens or fruit salads.

Mozzarella was made at the salumeria and it was always fresh, in water and the size of very large eggs. It was spooned out of the water, wrapped in waxed paper and eaten as soon as you brought it home. I didn't know it, but I was a gourmet in training.

I walked to all the stores. I talked to the shopkeepers who were paesani or friends, sometimes in Italian. I paid cash, counted my change, and on the way home, I was allowed to give myself a tip. It was usually an Italian lemon ice, from the pastry shop, in a soft pleated squeeze cup for five or seven cents. What a memorable taste!

"Going to the store" used to be an epicurean adventure through the Italian neighborhood.

LET'S SING AGAIN!

I pledge allegiance to the flag every day, not because I am so patriotic but because I work in a school and the pledge is led over the loudspeaker every morning. I rarely hear the Star Spangled Banner follow the pledge because the opinion is that our national anthem is too difficult. I admit that as a student I'd slur the words, but eventually I learned to say each word and understand the meaning of the phrases. Sometimes we sang "My Country Tis of thee"(America) but it seems we've been lax in teaching our patriotic songs lately.

I remember formal assembly programs when I was in public school. The entire student body sang the patriotic songs we learned during music class. We wore assembly dress, blue skirt\pants, white blouse, red tie. We stood at attention as the flag was carried down the aisle onto the stage and stood tall as we sang.

We were required to memorize the words of many patriotic songs and sing them on demand. Most kids knew the parody of "The Battle Hymn of the Republic " and the authentic words.

"Glory Glory Hallelujah, Teacher hit me with a ruler," was enough to get the music teacher into a frenzy and have your mother called up to school.

Irving Berlin wrote "God Bless America" and I don't know if Kate Smith made the song famous or "God Bless America" made her a celebrity, but I do know that tears came to your eyes when she sang.

We have to sing again! We have to sing about our country to help resurrect patriotism in our society, beginning with our children. I remember singing the armed forces songs," Anchors Aweigh," and the Marine Corps theme and learning who "Montezuma" was and where the "shores of Tripoli" were, because of the song. The neighborhood kids sang revelry.

"You got to get up, you got to get up, you got to get up in the morning." We stamped our feet and marched to the beat.

We sang "Yankee Doodle," "Columbia the Gem of the Ocean," "When Johnny Comes Marching Home Again," and "Dixie. We loved Roy Rogers' cowboy "national anthem," "Home on the Range."

Recently Lee Greenwood, country music star recalled his latest concert at the Twin Towers and the joy of everyone joining him in his hit "God Bless the USA."

"America the Beautiful " is still my favorite. The description of our country in song is inspirational, as is the finale in most Independence Day concerts, Sousa's "Stars and Stripes Forever." I feel like standing up and shouting "Hurray", after that piece.

There are many immigrant children in my school and Woody Guthrie's "This Land is Your Land" is appropriate in welcoming new arrivals to America.

Let's sing for the safety of the USA. Let's sing about the beauty and freedom of our great country. Let's sing to heal our sad hearts. Let's all sing- especially "NEW YORK, NEW YORK," loud and clear.

VENEZIA VS VENICE

Venice is one of my favorite Italian cities. It is unique with historic palazzi along canals and those distinctive black boats that date back from medieval times. I remember a summer evening long ago when a gondolier wearing a striped shirt and straw hat sang to me and I became enchanted with the city known as "La Serenissima".

I always enjoy walking over the labyrinth of bridges and getting lost in the maze of alleys called "calli". They are narrow and spooky, and make me think a masked figure might appear at any moment. That could very well happen during the world famous Carnevale in Venezia. The celebrations with masks, costumes, musicians, jesters, and parades are a last fling of fun before the solemnity of the Lenten season. The famous traditional white masks of "Bauta" or the beak nose "Medico" can disguise a prince or a pauper's antics in Piazza San Marco!

I just returned from Venice, but not the Venezia of gondolas, Doges Palace, St Mark's Square, and Rialto Bridge but, Venice, California, with Muscle Beach, surfboards, roller blades, bike paths and carnival atmosphere all year long! Venice Beach is my new favorite place in the world because my son and his wife live there and recently blessed me with a "Venetian" grandson.

Influenced by a memorable trip to Italy in the early 1900's, a man named Abbot Kinney aimed to make a replica of Venice as a seaside resort for prospectors in Southern California. The simple layout of straight canals dredged out of the swamp are connected by bridges just high enough for the water traffic of canoes, kayaks, paddles boats and ducks.

Shrubs and vibrant flowers border the canals of swift moving water routed from the Pacific Ocean. Original quaint cottages are NOW reconstructed luxury homes for Hollywood types. The oceanfront promenade is a constant carnival with jugglers, clowns, loud music, glass walkers, and street artists.

Once in Venezia, I had to step aside to make way for an old man. To my dismay, he was pulling a wagon laden with a wild boar and was headed for the kitchen of a luxury hotel. I did not have dinner there that evening. In Venezia, I try to glimpse through iron gates and portals, which may lead me to a church that contains a Titian or Tintoretto masterpiece painting from the 1500s. As I meander along the walkways and dodge skateboards in California, the most I can hope for is a pedigree dog on the leash of a famous actor or an outdoor mural tribute to a 60's rock star.

The overhanging smog on the West coast shadows the sun until noon but lacks the mystique created by the morning veil of mist over the lagoon and canals in Italy. When I stop to look up at the Ponte dei Sospiri, I think of the prisoners who shuffled from the judicial chambers on one side, to incarceration in the dungeons across the bridge. They sighed at their last view of beautiful Venezia, hence the name Bridge of Sighs. I too, sigh when I leave Venice because I know it will be a while until I return to play with my grandson.

Now I have two favorite Venices to visit, although, my personal compass has a stronger magnet force in Venice Beach. I hope that one day I will enjoy a gondola ride, during Carnevale with my California grandson, in Venezia.

Venezia and Venice Canals.

WHO DIED?

I come from a family of funeral directors, or as they used to be called undertakers, morticians or "beccamorti" in Sicilian! Three nephews, my brother-in-law and my SISTER are licensed embalmers and funeral directors. Despite my exposure, I'm still squeamish when viewing a corpse lying in a coffin.

Over the years, my neighbors have not been aware that the unassuming station wagon parked on my driveway was occupied by two dead bodies! While my relatives stopped for a quick coffee, my sons would announce the unusual cargo and soon their friends would gather on my driveway. Peering into the windows of the car, they would make ghost sounds, trying to wake the dead and were probably expecting Frankenstein.

My daughter once wrote a morbid report that worried her fifth grade teacher. I'll never forget the teacher's expression of disbelief when I explained that the detailed description of the morgue, was correct. My sweet little girl had visited the morgue with her aunt on business. I'd probably be brought up on child abuse charges for this today.

I think my first visit to a funeral home was for a school mate who had died from a childhood disease. He lay in the coffin wearing his first communion suit, hair slicked, clean face, angelic as I had never seen him before. Another time I viewed a neighbor dressed in her wedding gown and veil, surrounded by floral arrangements called Gate of eaven and Bleeding Heart

There was a time when wakes were held in the home. I can still conjure the macabre image of a young man in the casket in the alcove of the family's parlor. The windows were all around with sheer white curtains over Venetian blinds that let in just enough light to make it eerie. Many relatives, dressed in black, kept a vigil. That image comes every time I pass that house today.

Funerals are a sad but necessary part of every culture. Each ethnicity has its way of saying good bye. I witnessed a cremation on the Ganges River of India as the oldest son fed the pyre of his parent. I've paid condolence calls to my Jewish friends during their week of mourning at home. I've attended Irish funerals where prayer and cheer helped the grieving family. Italians become emotional but they are always hungry, so there used to be kitchens in the basement of the funeral homes where comfort food(pasta)could be cooked. The Board of Health put an end to that years ago. Now, collations are held after the funeral in a nearby restaurant or a relatives home.

Families sometimes make unusual requests, such as a daily change of shirt for the departed (as was his custom in life). Some corpses wear eyeglasses, not because they still need them but because acquaintances might not recognize them without their specs.

Did you ever see a horse at the cemetery" Well, "Biondino" was commissioned to attend his master's funeral and for good reason. In the later stages of Alzheimer's disease, the demised gentleman had periods of lucidity only when he visited the stable and Biondino's stall. The funeral director was accommodating but tense while the horse paid his respects!

In Italian neighborhoods, on the day of the burial, the length of the cortege provided prestige. Three flower cars or more meant you were a big shot or you had a lot of cousins. The slow procession passing the house as a final good bye, and removing the door flowers, were a heart wrenching scene.

It used to be that the friends gathered quietly, went up to the casket, said a prayer and sat a while to comfort the family. Now wakes remind me of a cocktail party. There are no row of chairs and everyone seems to congregate in the back of the chapel. Some never even look at the deceased. Picture boards are displayed, and after two days and a short mass the person is put to rest.

I used to laugh at older folks reading the obituary columns to see who died. I'm starting to show my age because, "guess who" reads the obits everyday now and says, "Thank God, my name is not here today!"

79

BLOWING IN THE WIND

They've banned outdoor clotheslines in an elite small town in New York because they create "aesthetic pollution!"

What is this world coming to? Clotheslines have character! Who can forget the scene in an Italian movie of Sophia Loren bouncing down a narrow street in Naples under a canopy of swaying wash?

The laundry was still there the last time I was in the Santa Lucia area near the bay. The clotheslines were strung "palazzo" to "palazzo" across the narrow alley with a few garments that were gray from car fumes. I think they pay the residents to hang their wash out so tourists can capture a "Kodak moment!"

I remember my godmother using a wooden wash board to scrub clothes in a deep wash tub next to the kitchen sink. She used a bar of brown Octagon soap, and added Givel. The "Biancolino" man delivered huge containers of this liquid bleach once a week. I'll never understand why a blue substance was then diluted into the rinse water. Supposedly the scientific process of bleach and blue was to help the sun whiten the clothes.

Then the wash was put outdoors to dry. Most families hung the wet clothes on a line set up out a window on a pulley system attached to a pole in the backyard or the house next door.

A family's clothes line was also a source of gossip and information for your neighbors.

You could tell what a person did for a living. Work clothes and thick socks meant factory or construction work. White shirts meant business attire, school uniforms meant young children. You also knew who ate too much pasta!

The whiteness of your towels demonstrated domestic expertise and stained tablecloths meant they weren't scrubbed enough! The nosey neighbors also scrutinized the hanging method. Some people hung shirts from the shoulders others from the shirt tails, each insisting their method was the best for quick drying. Some folded sheets in half to catch the wind while others let them loose. You had to double up on clothes pins because they dropped off the line, got lost, and were never enough for the full wash. I thought wooden clothes pins were extinct but recently a friend told me she had saved some *crocchi* as a fond remembrance of her Sicilian grandmother. She also has the weathered sack that was hooked near the window to store the pins.

There was physics involved in hanging out the wash. Undies came first then larger items in the middle, and finally socks and smaller items again. The line was balanced and the sun and wind knew that. Sometimes the wind would billow through long johns and nightgowns and create a tarantella on the line to the music of the humming breeze. If a line broke and scattered your laundry you humbly went to a house on the next block to retrieve your personal items.

My family hung the wash on lines set up on a *terrazza*. When the wind twisted sheets and pillowcases around the line it caused wrinkles and that upset the household executive, my grandmother. She spied for rain clouds and tested for perfect dampness for ironing purposes. I remember the unmistakable scent of the clean outdoors on our "biancheria." Sprays and dryer sheets in today's machines cannot duplicate nature's fresh air bouquet. During the winter the clothes froze solid and created grotesque hard creatures, and of course didn't dry, but the routine was maintained anyway.

In the suburbs families used clothes umbrellas with plastic fasteners attached to the lines. Blackbirds sitting in nearby trees were ready to swoop down and dirty the wet clothing. Then some clothes had to be rewashed!

I also remember a huge standing loom with nails around the perimeter. Its special purpose was to dry and stretch hand crocheted tablecloths, bedspreads, and curtains that had been heavily starched That was a once a year project. The frame was put out in the sun and it was the original no ironing process.

Later a Chinese laundry opened in the neighborhood and spendthrifts had their shirts and sheets washed and ironed there. They were returned wrapped in brown paper. That was a luxury for some people long ago.

Dry cleaners were available but used mainly for heavy coats. We used a cleaner called Carbona for home spot cleaning. Now one little spot and the garment goes into the car trunk for the next visit to the cleaners. That's life, that's progress.

Smelling the jasmine in Taormina

The Women (in America)

Women in America essays celebrate our mothers, sisters, grandmothers, and aunts, as carriers of the culture. They developed new roles in America, adapted, and enjoyed their budding identity. Women's subtle influences such as *batti manine, pastina,* use of Italian words, and routines in the home, insured the persistence of ancestral values and traditions. They became sentinels with a great responsibility for Italian integrity, ideals, dignity, and courage.

Garden lessons

Blowing in the wind

Flora's *cappidduzzu*, age 3.

WORKING MOTHERS

"I'm a working mother" my daughter tells me very often and my heart breaks for her anguish. It's not easy to leave an adorable young child in someone else's care and concentrate on your profession. THEN I think back, did my mother, grandmother or neighbors work when I was a kid?

"OF COURSE NOT!"

My mother "helped out" in my father's store. A friend "greeted" guests at her family's restaurant. Other women took phone messages and did billing for their husband's plumbing or electrical services. Maintaining the home was their unsaid occupation but actually they were the unpaid workforce that helped build family businesses and professional offices. If anyone had asked my young children, "Does your mother work?" "Nah, she's a teacher," would have been their answer. The endless hours that I marked papers on the kitchen table (sometimes with their help) didn't count as work from their perspective. They saw teachers at school everyday and they weren't working!

I thought of the women years ago who had "little jobs" in the storefront factories that dotted my Italian American neighborhood. I recall the sound of power sewing machines humming and flowing out of open doors on warm spring days. The immigrant women walked to work after the kids were off to school and they had straightened out the house. They were home for lunch and then back again at three o'clock for the children's return- and to prepare dinner. That was the "little job" that probably paid for many "little things." and gave the women a chance to socialize with other women as well. Some of my friends' mothers brought home "piece work" to finish in the evening.

My godmother, Grace, however "went to business." She dressed stylishly with a hat and gloves, and carried a handbag that contained the tools of her trade. Her personal scissors was as important as a pen to a teacher. The subway commute to Manhattan validated the seamstress position as a real job. She made sample dresses for a famous designer of the time.

The bonus was she was able to get a few yards of the finest fabric from the end of the rolls and make dresses for herself and me.

I watched her make a white dress for me from triangular scraps of fine French eyelet. The "o's " in the words "cool" all over the material were the holes that created the eyelet. It was trimmed with delicate imported lace, also a remnant from the shop. One day I visited that big factory in the city and was impressed to see the long rows of "Singers." There was a huge table with layers of fabric piled high while a cutter was guiding the cutting blade around a pattern. I met the presser, the finisher, the designer, even a mannequin named "Bella," and got my first view of the fashion industry.

When I couldn't afford nursery school for my children I offered my teaching services and certification in exchange for tuition and we all went to pre-school together. I didn't work; I "played" with the kids. When summer camp was unaffordable again, I went with my kids and suffered through a season of 22 rain days with a group of twelve three year olds. These were "little jobs" and I survived!

NOW when my daughter says "I'm a working mother," my reply is, "I'm a working grandmother and so were your grandmother and great grandmother before that." It's a family tradition!

Teacher's helpers: My chuldren.

86

EMBROIDERY

Can you embroider? Does anyone know what embroidery is anymore?

When I was about eight years old, I was given a hoop and needles, colored thread and a small towel imprinted with a light blue design made of all "X's" and told to follow the lines. The needle had a blunt point and the fabric had a loose weave. It was sort of a beginner kit set up by my mother. But why did I have to do that?

I found out many years later on my honeymoon trip to Italy, and later still when I inherited the most magnificent sheets that my mother had designed and embroidered as a young girl as part of her trousseau. The sheets have a twelve inch border of intricate pulled thread and embroidery stitches that truly are fit for royalty bedding. They have survived many washings and years of memories. They were carried from across the ocean to Manhattan, then to the "suburb" of Brooklyn. Now they are on Long Island in my possession. Who knows where they will be next? The young people do not appear to appreciate the magnificence of their grandmother's youthful hopes and dreams sewn into the sheets and pillowcases that seem so old fashioned now. I hope they don't go into a garage sale! These are family heirlooms!

My little sampler was a first lesson in preserving the Italian tradition of monogramming linens and decorating "biancheria."

Making dowry pieces is so foreign to our way of life today. Brides just register at Bloomingdale's and choose what they would like as engagement or shower gifts. I still think that part of our culture is worth explaining to our children.

During my visit with relatives in Sicily I realized that the recreation for unmarried women was needle work. There were no discos or bar scenes in those days, here or there! I saw young women sitting in their doorways, where the air might flow and create a breeze, their backs to the street, busily working on beautiful tablecloths or towels. My aunt was the town embroidery teacher and was able to create designs even without sketching a pattern on the fabric. She duplicated real flowers and even created new species out of fine linen thread on unbleached cloth.

Much later colored thread, usually sent from America, was also used. The traditional pulled thread method called "Cinquecento"

(500) because of the five hundred threads in the weave of the fabric, was also passed on through generations. Different towns and areas of Italy had different styles of embroidery. In Tuscany, open work (intagliato) and embroidery were combined and in Venice, the finest lace was created.

I was born in Brooklyn and never knew my paternal grandmother, but her love was expressed by making the most delicately embroidered undershirts for me. They were so small they were able to be mailed, folded in letters. I used them on my daughter as an infant, who later used them on her dolls, and I still have some.

Although I was taught how to make French knots and petals on flowers with satin stitches, I did not develop the skill where the back and front were so much alike it was hard to tell the difference. I bear my aunt's name, Flavia, but did not inherit her talent. I can't create but I certainly can appreciate, and to this day I am partial to embroidered blouses, tablecloths, and even prefer a beautifully designed handkerchief to Kleenex!

DOWNSTAIRS

My house has a basement that is cluttered with "stuff" accumulated for thirty years. Each of my children tells me,

"Mom I don't live there anymore, but my stuff does."

Nobody wants it. I can barely make a path through their precious mementos, trophies, books, skateboards, rock star posters and a variety of junk. It must be a fire hazard and I don't even have a kitchen down there, although sometimes I wish I did.

I remember when the basement was the hub for the family. The basement kitchen was the hangout for Nonna or Zizzi most of the day. Coffee was on the stove, the radio was on, and a favorite saint was on a shelf overseeing everything. Downstairs was where they made and served those sumptuous healthy meals around a huge custom-made table. Once a year the relatives would gather around that work table to jar tomatoes or pickle eggplants, peppers or mushrooms.

The basement set up was similar in most of my friends' and relatives' houses. There was a serviceable stove with a single oven, a small refrigerator, a sink, and an oversized pranzo table that was always covered with a shiny checkered or floral oilcloth. Next to the sink was the perpetual dish rack on the drain board. In reality it was the storage shelf because with no dishwasher the cycle was from table, to sink, to drain board, and ready for the next meal!

We did not have colorful terrycloth dishtowels, but we had " la mappina!" My kids still call them "mappinas" but they missed the era when their grandmother would watch for the flour delivery at the bakery across the street and then be the first to ask the baker to save the flour sacks for her. The sacks were made of 100% cotton. My mother washed them many times to remove the flour emblem printed on the sack but there was always a faint image that remained. They were white, soft, absorbent, frayed at one end and of course free. The immigrants were resourceful.

A washing machine was later added to the utilitarian basement, but no dryer because they whisked the clothes out the back door for fresh air on the clothesline in the backyard. That entrance was usually accessible from the driveway as well. Only ankles and feet were visible from the basement windows but that was enough to identify who was home early from school or returning from work late. The front door was for company to enter "the museum" where they displayed the upstairs parlor with silk-upholstered couch, and Capo di Monte lamps like a furniture showroom. The chairs and couch were covered with clear plastic slipcovers that were very sticky in hot weather. Even the lampshades had a plastic cover. The upstairs kitchen was always shining like new because it was never used. Visitors were given a tour and led to the interior stairway down to the basement, to chat.

They sometimes partitioned the basement for a wine cellar area and the floor was painted cement. If you were lucky there was a lavatory down there so that you didn't have to climb two flights up to the marble bathroom. You only went upstairs to sleep.

The warmth of that basement kitchen was the heart and soul of many Italian American families. There was a lot of frying and baking done in those kitchens for the large families that incorporated unmarried or widowed aunts, cousins or newly arrived relatives from Italy.

My family did not have a basement kitchen. We had a "cucina" behind my father's store with essentially the same set up but we sat on wooden orange crates because there were never enough chairs for all of us. They were comfortable and sometimes sturdy and we survived. That's the way it was THEN! Is it still like that in some places NOW ? Maybe.

THE FUR COATS

There have been many unusual birds, ducks, toads and turtles in my backyard. They stayed outside. I also had uninvited guests INSIDE my house.

I was awakened by a scurry of squirrels in my attic one morning. They were jumping and dancing just above my bed and I thought they would certainly come through the ceiling. A roofer came to the rescue that same afternoon when my bushy tailed friends went out for lunch. My daughter called for help when she found an opossum in the garage. The police gave her the same advice I did. "Leave the door open and the opossum will go back to its mother!"

Then one night I thought burglars were banging my door down. I ran downstairs just in time to see a family of raccoons stroll past my sliding glass doors. It was two o'clock in the morning. My timed outdoor light had just gone out suggesting to the raccoons that it was no longer daylight. This family was living in my attic, rent free!

At daybreak I heard them come back and slip through the hole they made in my roof. At 7AM, I called 1 800 RACOONS and for $300 they trapped the critters and brought them back to the wild. When I saw one in a cage, I briefly considered using the thick pelt to make a hat to match my coat.

Wearing fur coats is not politically correct now but people have been wearing animal skins since cave days. It was fashionable in New York to wear fur coats in the late 40's and 50's. When the Italian immigrants of the 20's became prosperous because their small businesses were thriving, the families could indulge in some luxuries. The Italian ladies craved the status symbol of "una pelliccia." My mother and sisters fell into that category.

Those were glamorous years as I recall. There were weddings at the Astor and Commodore Hotels and people dressed up for the opera and Broadway shows. Groups of friends went to the famous nightclubs of the time: The El Morocco, Copacabana, and Stork Club, and a fur coat was an absolute necessity!

When it was time for my mother to be indulged with a fur she chose a curly black Persian lamb. I remember the day my mother brought the coat home, hung it on the door, and asked my father to look at her new coat. My father knew nothing about furs or spending money because he worked all the time. He was impressed with the monogram "Caterina" on the lining and then said:

"Non mi piace!" My mother was shocked. "You don't like it?"

"Mi piace meglio il marrone "

" Marrone," being the brown mink collar and cuffs. My mother would have loved an "all brown mink coat" but it was not in the budget at that time. The black fur, he said, reminded him of the color for mourning.

My sister had a soft brown mouton lamb coat when she was sixteen and my older sister had a fox jacket. I, the youngest, had a white rabbit fur muff and hand me downs!

Once, I sat behind a lady in church who was wearing a Stone Martins fur piece draped over a classic suit. I was mesmerized because five mink-like skins were attached and intact with paws and tails dangling, while the beady eyes starred at me! This was very unusual attire!

There is no doubt that fur coats keep you warm on cold wintry days, but I am afraid to wear my fur coat NOW because the animal activists may spray paint on me.

I should really wear a sign that says "trapped in my attic" because of my experiences.

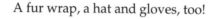

A fur wrap, a hat and gloves, too!

IL GREMBIALE

I remember when mothers wore a uniform - an apron. My mother wore one, my grandmother wore one, and all the aunts wore one. One neighbor was even buried with her favorite apron! No well dressed Mamma was without one. Long ago most women's daily attire consisted of simple house dresses. They were purchased in local dry goods stores or the house dress section of A&S or Macy's department stores. The basic style was short sleeve, button, snaps, or zipper up the front and a slightly varied neckline with piping or lace trim. The fabric was floral or patterned print, always washable and practical. With the ultimate Italian eye for fashion, the cover up apron was usually coordinated so as not to have a color clash.

My mother went through at least two dress changes per day when she helped my father in his store and since she was pleasantly plump her house dresses wore out in strategic places.

Then she became a recycling queen when she cut away the threadbare areas and created "un fallaru," (in Italian "un grembiale")- a.k.a. a front apron! Now, she could be creative and fanciful and add ruffles, a bow, rick rack or patch pockets to the colorful cotton. I think she could have rivaled Giorgio Armani with her designs.

Shirts too were salvaged for my father. When the collar frayed, it was ripped off, turned and reattached, exposing the newer reverse side for a few months more wash and wears.

The front apron was also very useful. It not only helped your house dress stay crisp and clean but when needed, the hem corners of the apron could be grasped to form an instant pouch for holding anything from string beans, sorted socks or clothes pins.

So important was the apron phenomenon in that era that as a sixth grade sewing project all the girls had to make an institutional style white apron and hair cover for the 7th grade cooking class. Boys, were exempt from "apron construction" even though they might become famous chefs and restaurant owners in the future.

Today you may see men wear a comic theme apron and chef's hat when they are BBQ cooks. NOW, most busy Moms don't bother wearing an apron and, like me, have many stained blouses. Cobblers, dusters, mumus, seem to be a thing of the past.

But recently I had a surprise when I visited my friend Fran. On a special hook in her kitchen was a souvenir "Italy" apron hanging as a decoration. What a good idea! She says she really uses it. I am inspired. I will look for my "Ricordi di Sicila, Calabria, and Puglia" aprons and display then also.

I just might wear one over my jeans since the house dress craze is over. When I tighten those apron strings, I think I may feel closer to my Italian roots and memories.

Typical housedresses

"LE TRECCE"

I love my hairdresser. I like to think she is the only one who knows for sure...about my hair color and what hairstyle will flatter me.

My first hairdresser was my grandmother and she had the duty of braiding my hair every morning before I went to school. She made four braids then wove them together to portray one braid on each side of my head just like Margaret O'Brian's. I remember my Nonna pulling to make the braids tight and my complaining all the while. She would distract me by telling me stories about Italy.

She would tie bows on each end to match my pinafore and in hot weather my braids were pinned up for a Betty Grable upsweep. I always wanted curly hair so when the braids were undone and left ripples, I thought a miracle had happened and I was growing wavy hair.

Braids were for everyday, but banana curls were for special occasions, holidays, and Christmas. My wet hair was rolled in spiral fashion around strips of white cloth and tied at the scalp. The next morning, after an uncomfortable sleep the rags were removed and I had a full set of long springy curls hanging all around my head that lasted for a few days.

I went from braids to a pony tail in junior high school and when the rage was curly short hair, I had my first permanent. My hair was "electrocuted" by hot curlers attached to wires that hung from a Martian-like apparatus. The hair and foul smelling lotions sizzled and smoked for almost an hour and then "pronto," I had curly hair for six months.

Today immigrant children still wear braids. Recently a Mexican girl in my school had thick beautiful braids down her back. Her mother proudly explained it was not with three separations but four that made the interesting interlocking weave. Girls from India usually wear their long shiny black hair in one wide soft braid down their backs. Kids from the Caribbean islands sometimes have lots of little braids adorned with colored beads or beautiful clusters of thin, long braids, artistically placed around their faces. Recently I saw a teenage boy who had ten tiny braids standing up from his head in all directions. I counted them. His hair was parted so that stars were created on his scalp. I don't think his grandmother braided his hair early that morning.

I like braids and inspired by the movie "10", I did wear a braid as an adult for a few years. It was a hairpiece. I was told the hair was acquired in mountain villages of Italy because young women had natural healthy hair due to olive oil in their diet. The braided chignon was blended to match my own hair and fastened to the top of my head with large hairpins. The "tuppo" was quick, neat, and comfortable.

Now my weekly visit to the beauty salon is almost a religious experience. Women used to go to beauty parlors, men went to barbers with swirling poles in front. Now men can get hair styling in the chair next to me at a "unisex salon." My hairdresser is an Italian American with innate creative genius. She listens to my stories, and, does not pull my hair. She is my friend and is a better therapist!

Hail to the talented Italian American beauticians who over the years gave me feather bobs, paige boys, layered cuts, French twists, DAs, beehives, permanent and cold waves all for the sake of beauty. But braids by Nonna are still a very fond memory.

Banana curls all over.

96

CUTTING COUPONS

I admit it! I use coupons at the super market. Economics is not my "forte" but I try to shop for bargains.

I became thrifty by necessity when my four children were growing up. On the dreaded occasions that I had to take my kids shopping for food, I engaged their assistance. I set them loose in the supermarket with a few coupons in hand to get any cereal, juice, or cookies, they liked- as long as they matched a coupon.

My coupon awareness started many years ago when my mother saved "cupunee" (as she called them in her broken English). They were printed on Ronzoni and La Rosa maccheroni boxes. She tore them off the side of the box and even retrieved them from the trash if she forgot to clip them. It was a family endeavor, so I diligently trimmed them and made little packets of twenty-five thick paper coupons, fastened them with rubber bands and kept them in a drawer. We ate a lot of pasta, different varieties with vegetables or just plain garlic and oil every night, so the coupons added up quickly. When we had about 250 of them, we could exchange them for a gift.

I was commissioned to accompany my mother to the redemption center. She had a personal interpreter, me, and my role was to read the subway signs and ask directions in English. The small store downtown Brooklyn displayed just a few gifts on the shelves but it didn't matter. My mother aimed only for a good quality pot, pan, or "sculapasta" (I didn't know they called it a colander until I was a teenager)! It was something for nothing and she was satisfied.

NOW, out of habit I still cut coupons from magazines, newspapers, and advertising flyers, file them and usually forget to take them with me on shopping day. I wait for double and triple value coupon day specials, and the money substitutes expire!

Collecting Green Stamps was popular for a few years also. They were issued equal to the amount of your purchase. So you spent more money just to get more stamps. We pasted them into little books where the inferior glue rarely adhered. They were messy and I gave up on them.

Today's department store coupons seem to be a joke. They give you a 15% discount, only if you use your store charge card which then adds a 21% finance charge on the bill. It is a false savings and no bargain bonanza! I cannot believe Bloomingdale's and Nordstrom's don't issue coupons. Would you believe they honor Macy's coupons?

I can't keep up with it! It takes more time to cut and collate coupons than they are worth just to see deductions on the register tape of $6.52 or even as much $13.04(recently). Supermarkets issue and scan customer club cards for sale items but I think it really is a ploy to know what I eat for the year!

Computer generated custom coupons are currently available but the stores warn that they could be counterfeit. That could never happen with maccheroni box coupons years ago. The pasta was real, the blue, red, and yellow, box was real, and so was the coupon on it!

In Italy they call coupons "buoni" and are starting to become popular but the shopping style in small towns is different. They still buy fresh food daily in local stores and street vendors do not take coupons.

I am waiting for the BIG Italian coupon. When in Rome I will scour every newspaper and magazine for a discount voucher for a Fendi, Prada, or Gucci purchase. I guess I will be there for a while. NOW that would be a coupon worth clipping!

FAMILY FEUDS

Italian American families are generally thought of as large, happy, intact, families. If it's your family you can laugh because you know about the underlying dysfunctional element that many families experience.

Everyone knows Uncle Tuddi doesn't talk to Uncle Jim, and Aunt Vera and Aunt Rosa have not made eye contact in years(but each knows exactly what the other wore to the last wedding they attended)! If you ask, "Why don't you talk to each other?" Truthfully, each party would say the same thing. "I don't remember!"

Who hasn't experienced the tension in the air when two embittered members of the family are in the same room? Years of silence just slip by and the anger drifts to indifference. The rest of the family tolerates the fracas and learns to maneuver around the situation. You can be told, "Be sure your two uncles are not seated facing each other at the baptism party." If you dare exclude a person from the guest list, then you'll start another feud! You just can't win! This stubbornness and animosity wastes our most precious irreplaceable commodity, TIME.

I knew two sisters whose husbands had not spoken to each other since they were in their twenties. The sisters were expected to be supportive of their husbands' bad feelings. Instead, over the years the sisters enjoyed a special relationship. They had lunch together once a week, went shopping and even baked holiday cookies together, all unbeknownst to their husbands- the staunch enemies. The power struggle remained until death, when the survivor attended the other's funeral -for respect and not to make "mala figura." The public reconciliation was too late.

I think my family had the ultimate feud! I grew up living with Mamma, Papa, two sisters, a brother and my maternal grandmother. But where was my grandfather? He was alive and well but banished from Brooklyn, by my grandmother, to an island for life! (Staten Island). After many years I found out why my grandmother muttered under her breath every time she saw my grandfather.

The story is told that my grandmother, Caterina, was a blue eyed, light haired, spirited beauty. In 1901 in Sicily she was engaged to be married, not to my grandfather! No problem. He, with his cousin as an accomplice, entered Caterina's house while she was washing the floor and literally carried her away. As they swept her off her feet, like Cinderella, she left a shoe behind. My grandfather's name was Angelo, but obviously he was no angel. My mother was born in 1902. My grandmother hated him for the rest of her life.

NOW the kidnapping would be punishable by incarceration, but THEN it was common practice in Italy!

Angelo came to America and dutifully sent for his wife and two children. They tried living together and operated a grocery store in Queens, but my grandmother, a clean fanatic, vehemently hated him and his pet white mice! So my grandmother lived with us and consequently I did not know my grandfather well. How sad that so much energy is exerted to maintain hate when loving is so much easier.

Some couples after divorce never speak to each other again despite having created beautiful families together. What kind of example are we setting for the next generation if we are not talking to our blood relatives because of jealousy, inheritances, or children's fights? How can there be peace in the world if we can't have peace in our own families? PAX, PACE, PEACE, one person at a time.

The *carrettino siciliano* in Erice.

THE BABY SHOWER

I recently attended a baby shower. Forty women of all ages, gathered to wish the pregnant mother well, and shower her with gifts for her unborn child- a boy, to be born on a specific date named Matthew and approximately 7lbs 6ozs. There would be no surprises except perhaps the color of his hair, if any!

It sounded like science fiction to me. I'm from the era when old wives tales told you the baby's sex by the shape of your body and more scientific experiments and data like sitting on a spoon or how sleepy you were. When the gifts were opened I definitely felt like a visitor from outer space.

"What is a wipe warmer?" I asked.

"Oh, that's a little electric heater that keeps the disposable wash cloths warm so that the baby does not shiver during a diaper change." In my day, Mama's warm lips just kissed the baby's bottom, a little baby oil on a cotton ball made the baby smile and all was well.

Now the diaper compactor is a great invention! I really could have used that when I had three kids in diapers at the same time.

Years ago we washed and reused cloth diapers-sometimes even boiled them to get them white. After my child got a severe diaper rash and I was ordered to paint his buttocks with a purple substance I quit and called the rescue squad, diaper service with delivery twice a week!

"Huggies" in my day were just that- arms around mama's neck!

Unlike the tape tabs on disposables now, we used large safety pins to secure the diapers and each time the baby cried we were sure one had opened and was pinching the infant. No swim diapers. colorful or sleep sizes then. We put double and triple diapers on at night and then tight rubber pants! Poor babies.

We didn't have baby showers years ago. Italians believed nothing should be in the house for the expected child. It was bad luck.

However, each set of grandparents tried to outdo the other by providing everything the newborn needed before the baby came home from the hospital.

They provided status symbol coach baby carriages (white or navy blue) with large wheels and springs for the baby brigade through the neighborhood. Monogrammed plush comforters or hand crocheted covers, fit for royalty, kept the baby warm during the daily walk. No baby left the house until they were baptized.

I love the new light umbrella strollers. I remember perforated metal "kiddy cars," with tiny wheels close to the ground and vaguely, the clumsy summer wicker strollers. What a difference!

Highchairs, cribs and play pen were the other basics gifts from the family. Some high chairs had a potty in them. The baby sat until the deed was done and every mother swore the baby was trained at eight months.Who was trained Mom or babe? We didn't have our homes baby proofed. We had small apartments and grandma had RADAR. She usually lived downstairs and knew what was going on and insured safety. Crawling babies spent a lot of time in a playpen and toddlers could be traced by the bells on their shoes when the little anglers went fishing in the bathroom.

We didn't have TV monitors or car seats. We used two telephone books as booster seats and before musical swings grandma, grandpa or an old aunt cradled the baby in their arms and sang them a lullaby until one of them fell asleep.

Gone are the doggie proppers, bottle sterilizers, white shoe polish, belly bands, rubber pants, carriage harnesses, and Foley food strainer. Those were the days!

There is a whole new vocabulary and marketing audience for babies. Now when they find a short cut for the 2AM feeding, I will certainly be impressed.

SPRING CLEANING

I welcome sweet springtime with the warmer temperatures and longer daylight hours but I do not look forward to spring cleaning! I really should not complain because I get help from a cleaning service. A team comes to my house with equipment and products unbeknown to us years ago.

Although the Fuller Brush man sold us string mops, dust mops, and feather dusters, our old clothes made better cleaning rags. I remember my grandmother using an old towel guided by a broomstick (as they did in Italy) to clean the linoleum floor in our kitchen. Then she placed sheets of newspaper as stepping spots to keep the floor free of footprints for a while longer. I can still remember the smell of the CN solution we used on the floors and to clean the bathroom. We were convinced the medicinal scent made it a genuine disinfectant

Recently a friend removed some carpeting and discovered beautiful parquet hidden for 68 years in her old Brooklyn house. Years ago we used wool area rugs and only the beautiful wood border was exposed. Every spring we rolled up the rugs, hung them outside and took out our frustrations with a twisted wire rug beater to extract the winter's dust and dirt. A woven straw rug filled the center of the living room for warm weather.

Spring was the time to lemon oil the furniture, let the sun and fresh air in and the parish priest also on his yearly visit during Lent to bless the houses. That was the deadline set to have everything in order.

We dangled blankets and pillows from the windows to "air out" while the rooms were being prepared for the season's conversion .

I don't know who wrote "the law" that said we had to change the curtains but every April down came the dark brocade drapes and up went the thin curtains. Floral prints were everywhere, slipcovers, bedspreads, tablecloths. Spring was coming.

But before the window coverings were changed, the winter's residue had to be removed from the outside of the windows. This was a chore that required the balance of an acrobat and nerves of steel at my house because we lived on the second floor and I had to sit out the window to wash the glass panes. I remember actually sitting on the sill with the lower sash of the window closed and compressing my thighs and the steel track digging into the back of my upper legs. My backside hung over the sidewalk fifteen feet above the ground and my grandmother would hold my knees for balance as she criticized my streaking of the glass. We used newspaper and straight ammonia or vinegar that could asphyxiate you and have you tumble out in a flash. No wonder window washers use a scaffold and a safety harness, today.

Most people had Venetian blinds, THEN, that had to be cleaned. I'm convinced that each slat was a magnet for dust. A decorator told me they are fashionable today and recommended them for my family room.

"Oh, no!" I protested "I am not interested, I still remember soaking and scrubbing them in the bathtub years ago." If I want anything Venetian I will go to Venice." I may have to relent.

Every year one neighbor removed all the natural wool stuffing from the dowry mattresses she brought from "il paese." She washed the wool by hand then placed it on flat surfaces to dry in the sun. I watched her as she used two hands to stretch each and every curl of wool and created a small hill of fluff. She would struggle to re-stuff the clean blue striped linings until they were plump and full.

My spring cleaning is easy NOW. I have twenty-three windows in my house so I call a window washer once a year. I certainly do not change my window treatments until they are ready to be replaced! I don't know what is in my mattress. My oven is self cleaning and my refrigerator is frost free. My mother never owned a vacuum cleaner but my daughter has a central vacuum system with an outlet in every room. I have an upstairs and a downstairs vacuum cleaner but I would really like one of the new little robots that scoot about the room searching for dirt by itself. Maybe I'll hint so that I'll get one for my birthday!

HIGH TECH

I am delighted to participate in today's technological progress. Computers, microwaves, phone cameras, space travels are all good things- I think?

But I get into a dilemma every time I go to my children's homes to babysit. Each phone has a different connectivity device and worst of all I can't get their televisions to work!

What used to be a simple task of turning a knob one twist to the right has become a multi step process that requires a manual created by engineers. It used to be so simple- two dials one for on/off the other for sound level, then the picture tube lit up and you could relax. Now you need three command sticks to view a menu. There is a control for the TV, DVD, and the VCR. What do those letters stand for anyway? There is also an adaptor for the game cube. Since Satellite and Cable TV are not compatible, that requires another switch. I don't know which to activate first so I usually start mumbling.

"Ma come si fa?"

In desperation I ask my grandson, "How do we get the TV on?"

"I don't know. Mommy says don't touch it?"

I push a few buttons at random and the home theater system kicks in. The around sound booms; it feels like an earthquake and startles me. When the menu does appear there are 200 listings with nothing that interests me!

I dare the entertainment center to a technical duel and I hope to win. I decided to record my favorite show "Visions of Italy." I diligently followed each step of the directions. I set the channel, timer, date and pushed the VCR record button and went out. When I returned, I found an Asian news show and an unmentionable program on my tape! My handicap was confirmed. I am technically challenged! NOW, I am told VCRSs are almost obsolete anyway. TIVO is in. So what's next? We can get movies on demand and also change the language. We can keep track of a sports event with a small screen within a screen. There are huge blow up TV screens to use at pool side.

The TV vocabulary has me baffled. Plasma has nothing to do with blood. Does HD for high definition mean I do not need my glasses to watch the Italian cooking shows? What is a projection, wide screen or LED set?

I would love to have a modern flat screen TV hanging on my den wall, but they tell me that the life span of that type of TV may only be about three years. That is crazy! It would take me that long to learn how to use it. I recently donated an old 13 inch black and white television (with knobs) that had been around for a long time and it still worked.

This is simply too much home entertainment and high tech for me. I think I'll just take the kids to the multiplex!

No high tech for gelato in Siracusa.

HOME REMEDIES

Recently a friend gave me a beautiful tin box filled with herbal teas. It contained tea bags of exotic flavors, - mango, kiwi, passion fruit, almond, etc. So where were my grandmother's favorites, - fennel, chamomile and bay leaf flavors?

I remember when the remedy for headaches, stomach ailments and melancholy was a cup of weak tea brewed with some herbs. Chamomile helped you sleep; bay leaf or fennel could be diuretics and helped you digest. You sipped slowly and relief came quickly. I think the Italian immigrants were ahead of the times with alternative medicine.

When my daughter was born at 4 pounds, and was finally brought home from the hospital at 5 pounds, it seemed she cried all the time. I was advised to give her a weak tea made with fennel seeds. This was long before there were natural food stores so I bought the seeds at the pork store. I made the potion and fed it to my infant. I was desperate. It worked! She slept like a baby!

There were many natural treatments for whatever ailed you when I was young. You hardly ever went to the doctor's office. If you did visit the doctor you were likely to wait a very long time until the overworked physician popped out of the examining room, escorted the patient out to the waiting room and said "next." There were no nurses, no insurance forms and you paid cash, if at all. A single doctor knew everything. He was Gynecologist, Pediatrician, Dermatologist, Cardiologist, and Psychiatrist!

There was a time when a belly ache might be called a "dirty stomach" and of course a laxative was prescribed. You had "scarola" soup with a dot of olive oil and that cured you fast. Plain boiled escarole worked every time.

Olive oil was an all purpose staple. A drop of warm olive oil in an earache and a little massage around the mastoid area quickly relieved the pain. Olive oil was used for everything from dry scalp to helping fade a scar.

Lemons were in abundance in Italy; toothpaste did not exist. So my grandmother used a mouthwash of lemons, salt and water to keep her gums healthy and her teeth white. It worked.

I vaguely recall an unusual practice for lung and respiratory difficulties. A silver quarter, our American currency, was placed on the chest (or back) with a small square of cloth. Then the cloth was lit with a match and quickly covered with a thick shot glass. The smoke was contained in the glass. A vacuum was created; the skin rose and as the smoke cleared so did the lung problem. It seems sinister but they tell me it worked!

Rashes were cured with egg whites brushed on the area. It cooled and tightened the skin immediately and relieved the itch. It worked! Now an egg white facial is high priced at a spa.

Some old women would knit a woolen "fascia" or" sciarpa" to wear on their painful arthritic knees or elbows. Good lamb's wool was warm and worked wonders! Even today my friends in Italy wear a scarf because "la corrente" (a draft) can give you a sore throat or worse.

I had a relative who was a "pseudo chiropractor." He was summoned for back rubs and neck adjustments and then stayed for dinner. They said he had "healing hands" but actually he worked as a presser in a factory all week and I suppose his hands were perpetually warm! That was the touch that rid someone of a pain in the neck!

Many people had a skill. One of our neighbors was a midwife and a cousin knew how to swab your throat with iodine if white spots were visible. Today you take antibiotics for ten days and a culture goes to the lab.

We run to a "specialist" for diagnostic tests as soon as we perceive a symptom NOW. Years ago no one knew their cholesterol levels or blood pressure. They didn't even know their weight! But surely Italians knew red wine was good for you. The best cure must have been a glass of wine because to this day, we hold up a glass and toast, "TO YOUR HEALTH, SALUTE"

MALOCCHIO

Malocchio literally means bad eye. In my mind that could be amblyopia, pink eye or any disease curable by an ophthalmologist - but not in Italian tradition. *Malocchio* was taken seriously by the superstitious. *Malocchio* is the "evil eye" and it can be cast unknowingly on anyone, children and women being the most susceptible.

It seems years ago every family had someone with special powers. The "gift" was passed down secretly through the generations to a grandmother, aunt or distant relative. They had "the eye" under those bushy eyebrows to discern what was supernatural, and they knew ways to avoid or expel "the hex." The provocation for a curse was just pure envy about anything: beauty, advantage, property.

Precautions were taken to insure a safe and happy home. A new broom, salt, and coins were the first things brought into a house. A horseshoe might be hung over the threshold as protection from strangers. Hanging a garlic braid was not only ornamental and edible but it was to help repel any bad vibes. The braid also supplied the garlic cloves that some kids wore in a pouch around their necks, just to play it safe.

Any new car needed a big red bow on the rear view mirror. It didn't matter if it obstructed the view. The bow would bring good luck, especially if it was enhanced with a St. Christopher medal!

We put a little red bow somewhere in a baby's crib or carriage in case someone said "What a beautiful baby!" and didn't mean it.

If a child was particularly fussy for a prolonged time, colic was never considered. Someone with "the gift" was asked for advice. A good witch performed a foolproof test to determine if the child had been overlooked. First she made the sign of the cross on the child's forehead with olive oil. Then three drops of oil were dropped into a bowl of water. She blew on the water and then observed the movement of the oil droplets. If the drops floated independently there was a *malocchio* and a treatment began.

The child was held tightly to the chest over the shoulder. While rubbing the back, the healer whispered into the child's ear and intermittently yawned. With a mixture of prayers and unintelligible murmuring, occasional incantations to favorite saints, and deep breaths by the *malocchio* breaker, the baby would soon be calm, quiet, and asleep.

The follow up test was again with Italian olive oil. If the drops connected and looked like an eye in the water, the spell was broken, expunged, terminated. Salt was added to the water before discarded. I think a back rub and whispering in the ear might be helpful for me on my sleepless nights too!

For adult problems, like a severe headache, fatigue, or rash, they would tie a cloth napkin around the neck and have the headache victim sit, while the good witch sang and mumbled until she appeared to be in a trance. The person might begin to sway in her seat and soon the symptoms would be relieved.

I remember Italian men wearing a large gold or coral horn under their shirts (perhaps a gift when they left Italy to help Italian Americans ward off the evil Immigration Department). Then "il corno" became a fad and everyone, no matter what ethnicity, wore a gold horn. Only Italian Americans knew the real meaning of the amulet. I went through junior high school wearing a small gold horn on my bracelet but I think the only thing it did was keep the boys away.

My friend Marco, in Sicily, tells me if an emergency occurs, you could always make a hand symbol of horns (index and pinkie straight out, middle fingers tucked into palm, held down by thumb). It works just as well in times of fear or danger.

Years ago my book club read *Minnie Santangelo and the Evil Eye* by Anthony Mancini and the group giggled through the references to some of the beliefs we grew up with.

These ideas are not limited to Italians. My Greek friends have the blue eye charm, my Jewish friends spit over their shoulder three times to dismiss bad thoughts and the Chinese use Feng Shui to suggest the wall color for a room.

While *malocchio* is blamed for everything from headaches to earthquakes, it is an unusual tradition and part of our culture and folklore. NOW, I wear red a lot, I go in and out of the same door, I never walk under ladders, and I do not step on cracks in the sidewalks. I'm not taking any chances because I really don't know anyone who is bewitched.

A FAVORITE TEACHER

Starting a new school year is never easy for students, or teachers either! Ask any teacher and they will tell you about the school bells they hear in their dreams and the butterflies in their stomachs that begin in late summer. I'm included.

Today's students certainly are challenging and teachers' roles have changed. Since everybody has been through the education process, everyone has an opinion or memory about teachers. I can attest to the fact that some teachers had unusual behavioral styles in class. Some paced, some yelled, and some were so stern they made you cry. I still remember the names of each of my teachers from Kindergarten to 8th grade- in the correct sequence, and also the names of some of my catechism teachers. Those names were an enigma to me because the female nuns sometimes had names such as Mother Michael or Sister Gabriel.

Teachers usually remember the best students and try to forget the troublesome ones but everybody remembers their favorite teacher, the one that somehow reached, inspired or motivated you.

In my day it was Miss Savino. When I was a student at PS 216 most of the kids came from immigrant families. There was not one Italian American teacher for us to use as a role model until Miss Savino was assigned there. She was young, beautiful, had a contagious smile, and quickly became the most popular teacher. She was also an advocate for the study of Italian language and culture. She became Mrs. Alleva and somehow maintained a link to the neighborhood and her former students. She became the quintessential mentor and encouraged her associates to take exams for advancement. I later was able to call her "Paula" when I taught and she was the supervisor of Bilingual programs. She retired as a principal but not from her passion for helping Italian Americans. She has been honored by the US and Italian governments for her work. She instilled in her colleagues a sense of loyalty to organizations and commitment of service to help others.

When I was a kid I always loved school. My parents never went to teacher conferences or open school night because they didn't speak English well, but they got their information anyway! Fortunately my father's store was across the street from the school and the teachers came to my parents. While the teachers bought vegetables my mother had the opportunity to ask, "How my daughter do?" The reassurance that I was doing my work but was a "chiacchierona" (talkative) was enough information to get me grounded!

Teachers rarely know the effect they have on students. After pupils leave the school, teachers concentrate on the new kids. Once in a while you get a letter or meet someone and catch up on news and sometimes they say, "Thank you for changing my life" or "I remember that poem you taught us." These are the little rewards. I was lucky to have been touched by special teachers and I hope that I have been a favorite teacher to some kids. Paula Alleva influenced a multitude of young people and continues to do so today. Thanks Paula!

Paula Savino Alleva (left end).

112

THE GYM

My doctor's mantra is "Exercise, exercise, exercise." So when I received an invitation for a trial membership to a local health club I decided to visit the establishment.

Immediately upon entering I felt intimidated. Some of the equipment looked torturous, but worst of all, I looked around and saw young svelte women wearing spandex mid-length shorts and bare midriff stretch halters and I knew I couldn't do that. I almost went into a panic. I didn't have the proper attire! I had planned on using my discolored sweats as cut offs. After all, my previous gym experience was as a student and every girl in the class had proper attire: an ugly green gym suit!

The collared shirt attached to balloon shorts had to be washed and ironed to pass inspection. My grandmother had diligently embroidered my last name across the back for quick identification by the teacher. I think that is where the NFL players got the idea to put their names on the back of their jerseys. My first name was on the pocket over my heart. It was one of the most unflattering outfits ever designed for human wear.

Boys were able to wear shorts and T shirts. Schools had two gymnasiums, a boys' gym and a girls', each of which was off limits to the other gender. Most times girls wore their gym suits under their clothes throughout the day to avoid the trauma of undressing at the benches that lined the gymnasium. Also, the rumor was that if you wore sneakers all day you could wind up with flat feet. So we tied them together and carried them to school over a shoulder. We wore them only for running on the highly shellacked wooden floor of the gym. We did jumping jacks, ran relay races and learned how to play volley ball. We practiced some basketball skills. Sometimes we were required to hang on ropes for an endurance test of 60 seconds that seemed like an eternity. I had the good fortune or "misfortune" to go to a high school that had a pool. One term of swimming was mandatory to graduate. I think it was spitefully scheduled for the first period when the water was ice cold. My hair was damp for the next seven periods. The school provided swimsuits for the girls. They were no shape, knit, one size fits all type, supposedly sterilized after each class, and also the color of the year: green. Boys were lucky. They swam naked!

Our grandparents did not need to go to a gym. They had jobs that provided all the muscle building exercise needed. Women maintained their small waists simply by walking everywhere.

I think our Italian ancestors were as fit as today's athletes, just by walking up the hills that we try to duplicate on our electric treadmills. They climbed real stairs, not stair masters, and ate lots of fruits and vegetables, as health food. They maintained low cholesterol and healthy hearts naturally.

I wonder if I spend my money on a six month stay in Italy rather than a six month membership to the gym, "Could I come back in shape, looking and feeling better?"

VICTORIA'S SECRET

Students get part time jobs. They may baby sit, lifeguard or deliver pizza. Most jobs have nothing to do with the career or profession they choose later. Summer and part time jobs are for developing work ethics, life experiences, and earning a little spending money. Some students get unusual jobs.

A dear friend of mine worked his way through Oswego College upstate New York at the Stardust Bra and Girdle Company. He was an engineering student and his duties required him to check the sewing machines so that they were in proper working order for the operators the next day. He also had to sweep the huge factory floor of lint, thread, and scraps. He worked at night and kept his job location a secret. He is a successful businessman today. I laughed when he told me. He felt sensitive about working in a ladies undergarment factory and insists that he never saw a finished product because everything was packaged by the end of the day. I can certainly identify with his embarassment.

Although no one in my family is named Victoria we did a have a secret. My mother wore a corset! I remember very well escorting her to the corset store! (I had to go everywhere to help read the signs) This was not a lingerie emporium like today's Italian designer La Perla, or upscale Great Shapes. The corset shop was clinical in appearance and busy because no immigrant woman went out of the house without the right foundation. The corset fitter proudly wore her tape measure draped around her neck as a symbol of authority. To be a corsetiere was a well respected skill years ago. I tried to be invisible while I waited. I usually buried my head in a book while I waited for her to have a fitting. Another OSIA member told me he waited outside for his Mom because as a twelve year old he was humiliated to be seen near an intimate apparel shop of unmentionables.

I remember thinking, "I never want to wear a flesh colored full toso harness like that."

The corsets looked tortuous with long bone stays, laces, grommets, and garters. The women swore corsets were good for posture, supporting stomach muscles (after childbirth) and some said it also helped in digestion by keeping the esophagus and upper body erect. Nothing sagged. Nothing jiggled.

115

Now a rock star wears a corset as outer wear or costume and young people emulate and enhance the style by wearing a bustier. Sometimes flesh tape holds everything together for plunging neck lines, revealing or scanty outfits, but everything jiggles anyway. With body spraying, belly piercing and slim waists there is no need for corsets any more. I think of my shy, modest mother with the corselet! What would she think now?

I went into Victoria's looking for the secret. I found frilly, lacy, tops and bottoms in all colors. While looking through racks, I saw a delicate polka dot chemise. Then I remembered, "I wore one of those until I was eleven. We called it 'una maglietta," an undershirt. Oh well!

Wedding night finery.

WHO TOLD OUR SECRETS?

The menu read "Tagliatelle with spring vegetables- $17.00".

"OK. Why not?" It was Las Vegas, spring and it sounded healthy. When the waitress served me I gasped, "That's my grandmother's *minestra di San Giuseppe* over pasta!" Peas, onions, artichoke hearts, asparagus, fennel, and my all time horror, FAVA beans, steamed together with olive oil. I couldn't imagine fava beans in an upscale restaurant called Sam's American. I asked to speak to the chef. He obligingly visited our table and told us indeed he came from Brooklyn, had a restaurant in Manhattan, but did NOT get the recipe from a mutual grandmother!

It's astonishing that our "casalinga" foods have made it to gourmet status. I'd like to know, "Who told our secrets?"

Recently, at a cafe, a tiny bowl of olive oil for dunking slices of crusty bread was placed on the table. It was reminiscent of years ago when piping hot loaves of bread were rushed home from the bakery with still steaming dough inside. It was drizzled with virgin olive oil so thick it was green, sprinkled with black pepper, perhaps an anchovy slipped in and eaten as a low cholesterol lunch. If I see "Olive Oil Sandwich" on any lunch menu, I might just order it.

I was raised having "cappuccino" every morning despite the adage that "children should not drink coffee". My mother and grandmother were immigrants so I ate what they had when they were growing up in Italy. It worked for them- they lived into their eighties. So I had strong black coffee, mixed with milk, heated in a small pot and biscotti (anise, salviati or sesame seed) dunked into a large cup of the brew and THAT was my continental breakfast. NOW, Starbucks charges $5.00 for the same thing.

Sundried tomatoes are in many recipes now, but I remember being on duty to chase bees and flies from the large white porcelain trays filled with tomatoes that my grandmother dried on our terrazza. Tomato paste was made this way also. My grandmother always complained that the sun in Sicily was hotter and better, and for the longest time I thought there were two suns in the solar system: one in NY and one in Italy.

Health stores now feature carob ice cream and candy as a chocolate substitute, but ask any Sicilian about "carrubbi" and they will

117

tell you they grow all over the island. My mother ate dried carob pods like candy, years ago.

Porcini mushrooms have been introduced to America but I remember when we ate wild mushrooms that were gathered in the woods. They were delicious but risky. I always ate them the second day when I knew if anyone had had a reaction from them-like dying.

It seems everyone now knows the word "gelato" it is almost synonymous with ice cream but of course a million times better. I can't believe I recently had fennel flavored ice cream. The secret that fennel eaten after a hearty meal helps digestion is not well known but to disguise it as ice cream was certainly creative.

I'm upset that pesto and tortellini have become mainstream. Tortellini were only for soup and pesto was homemade in August with hopes that it would last into November.

Who told about the healthy vegetables that we were forced to eat when we were kids because "They're good for you?"

"Pasta e fagioli" is now listed as Tuscan bean soup. "HA!" We all know what we called it on Friday nights. Broccoli rabe steamed with garlic now belongs to everyone (even if they mispronounce the name) and raw escarole in a salad is now considered gourmet.

I confess! I introduced batter fried zucchini flowers to students I chaperoned to Italy. They had trepidations the first time but the next evening they requested "those *fiori* things."

The long light green squash remains a bit of a secret although every part of it is healthy and edible. A soup was made from the most tender leaves (tennurini) with a mixture of different pasta shapes or a stew with the squash and lamb chops.

My favorite lunches when I was in high school were potato or peppers and eggs on Italian bread. The oil stained paper bag made it very obvious that I had an ethnic sandwich. Diner omelettes just are not the same.

Please don't tell any more. Let's keep some things sacred. Restaurants still do not serve toasted bread crumbs instead of cheese to sprinkle over pasta with fish sauces, or fried *cucuzza* on pasta with garlic and oil. I think ricotta salata grated on fresh tomato sauce, is holy and homemade rice balls are divine. SH!

Certainly don't tell about *capozzella* (lambs head served, eyes and all on a platter) or *Stigghioli* (intestines wrapped around herbs and cooked on an open fire). These may give the wrong impression. *Spiedini*, real ones, with rolled up pieces of veal and skewered with onion and bay leaf in between are too difficult to make, so you can tell about those. I guess we should be proud that our foods are so good that everyone wants to be Italian.

Recently I had an undercover lunch in Italy: pasta with sea urchins (*Rizzi*), *Neonati* patties, orange and olive salad, peaches in red wine, and a refreshing drink of water spiked with a drop of "zummu" (anise flavor). It was gourmet heaven!

Our Christmas Eve traditions are well known and featured in magazine articles but I think they will stay ours. Although the wonderful food we eat is envied I think only a real Italian American has a digestive system that has been fortified and can tolerate octopus, eel, squid, codfish, shrimp, sea urchins, calms mussels, anchovies, lobster, scallops, all at one meal, (and then be ready for meat the next day)! *Buon appetito!*

Looks like nonna's *strattu*.

PIERCING

I remember when I had my ears pierced. It was the fashion craze when I was in junior high school. I did not have my ears pierced as a baby because I am the youngest in my family and it was considered too ethnic and barbaric by my older sisters.

It was tradition to have infants' ears pierced at birth in Italy and the trend continued in America, I think to distinguish girl from boy babies. Both genders could be bald or have curly locks for many months, so hair was not a factor to determine the baby's sex - at first glance.

All the women in my family had pierced ears and wore beautiful coral, cameo, or aquamarine earrings from Italy. It was obvious that you were of Italian ancestry in my neighborhood if your ears were pierced. Mine were not. So, was I part of my family, Italian, Sicilian? Maybe I was adopted.

My sisters and cousin had their ears pierced when very young. Midwives or an aunt perforated the ear lobe of the baby girls within hours of leaving the womb, with no problem and barely a whimper from the infant. Tiny diamond studs were inserted and sparkled around chubby cheeks, and everyone knew it was a girl baby.

So when dangling earrings were the trend, I insisted that I too would be in fashion with holes in my ears. I did not go to a jewelry store where piercing was free, for the price of a pair of earrings, I went to a medical doctor, Dr Colombo, who put a sterilized needle through the fleshy part of each ear.

My ears were infected for weeks. Ugly black thread was looped through my ears and they were red and throbbed. When I finally had the black gut out of my ears I did not get diamond studs but little golden hoops, supposedly 14 k gold, not 18k Italian gold. I missed diamond studs THEN and still want them NOW.

Piercing and tattoos are a fad for both men and women today. Men with earrings had to be pirates in my day. Piercing of unusual parts of one's body does not appeal to me. The lip pierce gives me the jitters. Arrows through the eyebrow look painful, the tongue pierce is beyond my comprehension and finding my belly button has become difficult. I cannot fathom that a professional or CEO of a business would hire any pierced candidate. How do they respond to questions without a speech flaw?

120

Long ago, my oldest son went on a ski trip with his high school. When he returned, an entourage of teenagers escorted him into the house. I welcomed them home and the girls asked me to examine my son carefully. My face contorted with fear. Then he flashed his ear with a little heart dangling from it.

"Oh, no!"

They pierced his ear while at the ski lodge, with a sewing needle, no antiseptic, and no black string. My only comment was, "Thank God it is not a tattoo!" My rational being, a tattoo would be permanent but the hole in his ear would heal if he removed the earring.

I mean no offense to tattooed people; it is a free country. If you like them, go for it. I did toy with the idea myself one time of a little rose, a heart, or butterfly tattoo, when I was in a fit of rebellion. It would not have been easily visible on my body. I think I will have some family members guessing if, and where, I could be hiding it.

Cousins in Sicily.

A Terranova store in Sicily!

The Holidays (in America)

Holidays in America are the final link to our old customs and continue to identify us. We honor saints with outdoor feasts and traditional pastries. Holidays are associated with food, family, and religion. The emphasis on a food extravaganza for celebration remains strong and anchors the unique pleasure of being Italian for future generations. These memoirs pieces are true.

Will the Befana
come, too?

'Twas the week after Christmas.

THE MEMORY TREE

"O Christmas tree, O Christmas tree, how lovely are thy branches." I can sing that melody when I look at my tree because it is perfectly symmetrical, has plump branches and is a vivid green. It's not real! My tree looks like a real tree but it lacks the sweet evergreen scent, and the shedding pine needles. It magically appears from a box year after year.

I remember when my father sold live trees in front of his store during the Christmas season years ago. My whole family took turns staying outside to display them to potential buyers and to be sure "The Grinch" was not around. It was so cold that sometimes we started a fire in a metal pail to warm our hands. The Christmas season seemed colder THEN. We sent the fullest, tallest and best-shaped trees to decorate the church altar. There went the profits! In return, we did get a donation credit in the parish bulletin and many blessings from the priests and nuns. The remaining scrawny ones were given away free on Christmas Eve to any needy people we knew. I guess that was our silent Christmas spirit. Our own tree was usually the worst of the lot so when I had my own family, I was determined to have a big beautiful tree.

My first tree was a seven-foot " pure white evergreen!" It was supposed to represent a snow-covered spruce in the woods. To add to the confusion we used non-traditional blue and green shimmering ornaments, gold garlands and blue lights. It occupied half my living room for the whole month of December! We placed only unbreakable decorations on the lower limbs, not because the children might break them, but because the dog was curious and brushed under the tree causing havoc.

For a few years we did have a real tree, once cutting a tree from our own backyard. We gave up when we still found pine needles in the house in April and the tree became too dry to last until the Epiphany. Now, I look forward to decorating early. I put up my Christmas tree and presepio right after Thanksgiving, buy a can of pine scented spray and I am set until La Befana arrives!

My decorating theme is eclectic with many ornaments gathered during my travels, made by my children years ago, and more recently by my grandchildren. I reminisce as I hook on the old dough snowman, (a Scout's project) and the kindergarten collage ball. I reshape the foil wings of angels from my children's first grade. Then nostalgia creeps in and competes with the rhythm of the twinkling lights as my eyes get teary. My collection of Italian angels from the Florentine markets and the Roman catacombs are carefully placed beyond reach of little hands so that they may be heirlooms some day. My Venetian glass trinket shattered, but luckily I have a few tiny Sicilian carts hooked on branches to remind me of my roots.

I hang St. Francis plaques to remember visits to Assisi. The miniature framed Raffaello madonnas are from Urbino and little ceramic jugs from Gradara and Agrigento. My favorite memory comes to me as I pick up a small, silver, handcrafted "bambino." I bought it early one morning in Campo dei Fiori from a farmer who was also a talented artisan. Oh yes, I have an OSIA ball purchased at a convention and a Buon Natale ball someone gave me.

Although the adorned tree is not an old custom in Italy, some of my friends and relatives, who visited during the holidays are inspired to have small Christmas trees in their homes NOW. I wonder if they have New York souvenirs on them?

While dressing the tree is joyous, taking it down is such an ordeal that I am tempted to keep it up all year! Merry Christmas, *Buon Natale!*

The memory tree.

SOMETHING IS MISSING

Something is not quite right when I go to church. As my mind wanders during the too long homilies, I look around and realize something is missing!

There are no hats on any heads. I still can't believe no one wears a hat anymore! I remember when going to church was not only for spiritual comfort but also to show off your "Sunday best."

Females were obliged to have their heads covered when I was a teenager and, stylish hats fulfilled the obligation. And what hats they were!

I've worn everything from sequined kerchiefs to crocheted caps to wide brimmed horsehair picture hats the size of a small umbrella! In the 60's everyone wore "pillbox" hats- thanks to Audrey Hepburn and Jackie Kennedy starting the trend. My pillbox version was covered with white lilies of the valley and I think it attracted bees.

A few years earlier hats may have been decorated with a cluster of artificial cherries, a crushed poppy, cabbage rose, or colorful ribbon. A church sometimes looked like a garden of blooming flowers from the backpews.

During the ethnic phases French berets, high turban styles and even fur hats were popular. We wore felt hats adorned with feathers, brims turned up sailor style, or brims bent down cloche style. No hat was complete without an eye-catching hat pin.

I loved the intrigue of having a hat with an illusion veil to cover part of my face.

Later a mesh decorated with delicate bows, angora, or sparkles that fit over your hair and face like a lampshade passed for a hat. Simple, but indeed a hat!

Men were obliged to remove their hats upon entering church and I saw many a fedora sat upon as it lay on the pew in front of me.

We wore hats summer and winter but in an emergency a handkerchief could be pinned to the back of your head with a bobby pin and served the same purpose. For a while I carried a lace mantilla for quick visits to my college chapel.

When hooded coats were the fashion, the hood substituted for a hat. Some seasons stocking caps or a colorful shawl, crisscrossed at the neck and thrown over the shoulders were the fads.

As spring approached you might see women caring a distinctive box from the best millinery shops, in preparation for Easter.

My girlfriends and I planned our Easter outfits for weeks "Are you getting a new suit or a new spring coat?" we would ask.

The operative word being "new". A new suit or coat meant new shoes, new handbag, new hat, and certainly new gloves to match.

While it was tradition to wear the previous year's outfit on Palm Sunday, we created a mini fashion show and neighborhood Easter parade "per Pasqua". I can't believe that I see people wearing jeans, sneakers, T shirts and shorts, in my parish. We wouldn't dare dress inappropriately for church years ago.

I miss those fabulous hats of yesteryear. I propose one Sunday of the month to be "dress up" and "hat day." Why did the patron saint of hats forsake us?

Buona Pasqua, and don't forget to wear your "cappeduzzu"!

RINGING IN THE NEW YEAR

When I put away the red and green decorations right after Christmas I start to think about the future and the new year resolutions I should make. Somehow they are always the same- to spend less money next Christmas and to start a diet, but not before Jan 1st because the theme for New Year's Eve is "Celebration."

I remember family gatherings on New Year's Eve when I was young. After a busy day at work and dinner we passed the last hours of the year playing cards or *Tombola* (Italian Bingo). When we heard the bells or the whistle at the station announcing midnight, out came the pots and pans, not to cook, but to make a racket. All the neighbors would run outside banging pots and pans with spoons. We used pot covers as symbols and created a symphony of noise. After a "Cin cin per un buon anno" with a homemade cordial or rock and rye we were in bed by 12:15 A.M.!

Now the saying "Natale con i tuoi e capo d'anno con chi vuoi" (Christmas with your family and New Years with whomever you want) prevails.

Many people get dressed up in with glimmering clothes and head for a lavish catering hall where for an outrageous amount of money you can dance, overeat, drink and be merry until the party's over at 4 A.M. You may even get breakfast and the newspaper before you go home. You get noisemakers that are not as loud as the clanging pots, and, because you are fortified by Bellinis or Cosmopolitans, you kiss everyone around you when the strobe lights and loud music announce midnight. The bonus is a headache the next day. What a way to start the new year. I think we were much more dignified years ago.

As a teenager, if you were allowed to go to a nearby party, you had to come home before midnight, kiss your parents and then you could return to the party until 12:30AM! Now I'm happy if I get a phone call from each of my children within the first twenty-four hours of the year!

With the advent of television, Guy Lombardo and his Royal Canadians signaled the new year by playing Auld Lang Syne at the Roosevelt Hotel in Manhattan. We watched the Times Square ball drop and then said "a domani."

For me even NOW it is not officially the next year until I see that ball drop in Times Square. The crowds there wait for the glass ball to descend and light up the numbers of the new year. I do too, in front of a TV. If I were jostled in that crowd, I would probably need a full twelve months to recover. Then thanks to satellite TV we can see the new year celebrations all over the world and wish everyone a "Happy New Year" for each world time zone, all night long.

In Northern Italy the custom is to be sure to be wear new red underwear on New Year's Eve. Red undies insure good fortune for the coming year. After a traditional dinner that includes sausage and lenticchie (lentils that symbolize coins), my friends in Bologna go to Piazza Maggiore with a bottle of Asti Spumante. As the old year burns in effigy as "il vecchione" and the new year rings in, corks pop and they applaud. Then the crowd scatters and the Italians go to private parties. One can imagine the antics to prove that indeed your friends are wearing anything from a red satin thong to red long johns! They must certainly start the future year in a jovial mood.

In Naples they tell me the tradition is to get rid of old stuff - even if it means out the window. I think many of us might want to do that in New York.

Now, at this point in my life I prefer to babysit for my grand-children on New Year's Eve, toast the future with a cup of hot choco-late and maybe wear my lucky red flannel pajamas. Happy New Year everyone!

'TWAS THE WEEK AFTER CHRISTMAS

It seems that every December, as soon as I see the department store decorations, the ghost of Christmas Past haunts me.

The combination of religious and traditional Christmas celebrations in Italian American homes have a mystique for the general population. Although our <u>eve</u> fish dinners have been glamorized, it is the special private family warmth that is difficult to explain to others. Family, food, and fun were the magic of Christmas and how I remember Natale.

Any (reasonable)wish was granted and no expense was spared to provide the Christmas meal. We fried sausage and "sfinge" after twelve and played *tombola* into the night.

THEN ,'twas the week after Christmas! We created another tradition. We went to RADIO CITY with our mothers, sisters, aunts, cousins, godmothers, anyone who was a responsible adult until we were teenagers and able to venture out by ourselves.

The trip was almost a pilgrimage and had a specific itinerary. A one hour subway ride for about 20 cents brought us to Rockefeller Center. We gaped in awe at the tallest tree we had ever seen and watched the skaters until our fingers were nearly frost bitten. Then we took refuge in St. Patrick's cathedral. We followed the line to view the elaborate "presepio" near the main altar. We removed our Christmas corsages from our coats and added them to the creche creating mountains of metallic color around the manger.

We walked across the street to Saks and were entertained by an animated Victorian Christmas village in the window.

All this was just a precursor to waiting on line to get into the great music hall. We waited for hours, sometimes four abreast, in a line that snaked around the block in the bitter cold.

When we finally did get into the theater, we walked up the grand staircase, our eyes tracing the pattern of the lush carpeting almost hyponotizing us. The Art Deco gold tone figures on the walls were bigger than life and seemed to greet us. We were almost "Deco" ourselves in fur trimmed coats and hat and maybe a muff, but we didn't know it at the time!

When we finally got into our seats we scanned the cavernous theater until the BOOM of the Wurlizter scared us into silence. The or-

131

ganist used his feet just as actively as his hands to play the gigantic pipe organ until the big screen lit up with the latest featured film.

Later, the stage show began with a procession of live animals and costumed characters. They formed a magnificent Nativity scene on stage! It was worth every moment waiting in the cold. Then the Rockettes' precision dancing, animal acts, acrobats and singers kept us in the holiday mood. The approximately four hour show was spectacular, all for the admission price of about $1.25.

The second best show in town was a short walk away at the ROXY theater It didn't have the Rockettes but it did have a ice show on a small rink on stage. Sometimes we returned to Manhattan another day to see that show as well.

After the show we were happy and hungry. We would walk down to Macy's and Lord and Taylor to enjoy their Christmas decorations. We waved at the live Ho-Ho-Ho Santa in Gimbel's window and headed for, where else, but Horn & Hardart's AUTOMAT!

After the sumptuous meals and leftovers we had been enjoying at home somehow a wall of little windows displaying sandwiches and desserts was still very appealing. The experience was unique. We needed lots of nickels. After we placed 4 or 5 nickels in a slot, the little window was unlocked and it released our gourmet choice: a brown oval casserole just big enough for one frankfurter and beans. Macaroni and cheese and fishcakes were also favorite choices. Dessert was a piece of the famous "less work for mother" apple or pumpkin pie.

We didn't get all of the material things and very expensive toys that are on the market today but we did gather as extended families and celebrate the "holyday." We hummed "Tu Scendi dalle Stelle" and sang "Silent Night." We always hoped for a white Christmas so we could walk to midnight mass while a glistening silent snow blanketed the ground. We preserved the sanctity of the season. Christmas was peaceful. I love Christmas.

Now, we order reserved seats for the Radio City Music Hall Christmas Spectacular. The live creche is maintained but there is no movie. I don't know what happened to the organ. The Chanukah and Quanza holidays are also celebrated in the show. The Roxy is history and the automats are gone.

I can still take my grandchildren on an abbreviated tour to see the tree and skaters, the cathedral and view the beautiful store windows but lunch in Central Park's Tavern on the Green amid a fairyland of lights will cost $50 each! *Buon Natale!*

ON THE FIRST DAY OF CHRISTMAS

The popular Christmas song begins with,"On the first day of Christmas my true love gave to me a Partridge in a pear tree." Every year 12 days before Christmas my mother gave to me "cuccia," "panelle" and no bread for lunch because December 13 was "la festa di Santa Lucia!"

St. Lucy, was martyred in 283 AD in Syracuse, Sicily when she had the audacity to reject a heathen nobleman's attention. Her eyes were gouged out for the rebuke and thus she became the patron saint of eyes. Today a macabre statue in the Duomo of Siracusa shows Santa Lucia holding a tray that contains her eyeballs.

The people of Sicily prayed to St. Lucy during a famine and THEN, miraculously, ships carrying wheat appeared in the harbor near the island of Ortigia. In thanks and as a devotion to Santa Lucia the people of Sicily traditionally fast from bread, pasta and wheat products on her feast day. It was the only day my father, not a religious man, relinquished pasta as "primo piatto" and had pangs of desire for fresh bread.

I helped my grandmother make panelle as a bread substitute. My job was to use a long wooden spoon to stir a pot containing a mixture of water and chickpeas, over a low flame, until my arms hurt! If it burned even slightly, I was in trouble. We spread the paste on the back of dishes and when it set, we cut it into triangles, then deep fried them. It was certainly an arduous and messy cooking lesson! NOW I go to a *focacceria* in Brooklyn and get perfectly shaped panelle, choose "cuccia con ceci"(grain soup with chickpeas) or with chocolate for dessert, and that is my loyalty and devotion to St. Lucy.

Every year I attempt to re-create the famine and abstain from bread on December 13th, if I remember! Predictably, I can expect a 6:00 A.M. call from my sister in Florida,

"Don't eat bread today. It's St. Lucy's day."

Later in the day I get another call from the other sister in Brooklyn.

"Did you eat bread today?" followed by,

"What DID you eat?" wanting a list of all food consumed so far. You would think St. Lucy gave them Weight Watcher leader status for the day.

"You can't eat corn muffins. Read the labels, they have flour in them. Have Rice Krispies instead." This is strict interpretation of a non-law.

"Give me a break!"

I thought Sicilians had an exclusive reverence to St. Lucy but I learned that St. Lucia is celebrated in Scandinavia also. She is considered the martyr that brought light to that country. Their celebration is very different from the Italian one. In Sweden the oldest daughter portrays the Queen of Light and wears a white dress, red sash and an evergreen crown with a ring of candles. They serve their families coffee cakes made with saffron because it is the golden color of sunlight. My daughter-in-law is part Swedish so maybe with the combination of Swedish and Sicilian blood my grandchildren might celebrate St. Lucy's day for me when I'm gone.

Although I am desperately trying to maintain traditions my children may just remember December 13 as one more of "mother's idiosyncrasies." I imagine them saying,

"Oh yes, there was a day my grandmother and mother didn't eat bread, When was that?"

"ON THE FIRST DAY OF CHRISTMAS," I'll shout from somewhere.

"ST LUCY'S DAY, THE SHORTEST DAY OF THE YEAR ON THE JULIAN CALENDAR"

But that's all they may recall. We are so Americanized.

St. Lucy's day has perfect timing. It always jolts me into the Christmas spirit and a panic because I should be wrapping the presents I haven't bought yet.

My consolation is that I do feel that it's official to start saying Merry Christmas for the next twelve days, so BUON NATALE and BUON ANNO, twelve times over.

St. Lucy's Day
Police, Caterina,
Flavia and
Antonina.

LA BEFANA

Santa comes to my house again, NOW, that I have grandchildren. But La Befana seems to be lost. Although millions of Italians migrated to our country, La Befana did not follow. Perhaps she needs Rudolph the red nosed reindeer to guide her.

The legend of the benevolent witch is that she creeps around the rooftops in Italy, swoops down chimneys, and leaves small gifts or coal in stockings depending on if the children have been naughty or nice. The Italian children await her arrival on the eve of January 6th just as American kids anticipate Santa Claus on Christmas eve.

Most parents perpetuate the Santa tradition by telling the children that they saw Santa Claus or heard reindeer hoofs on the roof and of course we have probably all tried the direct telephone line to the North Pole. Reading the classic poem "Twas the night before Christmas by Clement Moore, (that first appeared in the Troy NY Sentinal in 1823), confirms the legacy. The visions of sugar plums and a miniature sleigh with eight tiny reindeer and a little old driver shouting their names will dance in my head forever. I love Christmas. I love the family gathering, the food, the decorations, and the carols in both English and Italian. Tu Scendi dalle Stelle and Silent Night evoke emotions and memories of long ago.

Who can forget the Christmas eves of putting little red wagons, train sets and doll houses together, when our children were believers? The "easy to assemble directions" were written in Japanese and we would end up at three o'clock in the morning saying. "I think there is a part missing!"

We left cookies and milk out for Santa as an experiment, chocolate chip cookies and "cucciddati," to see which he liked best. Chocolate chips were the choice. La Befana would have eaten the fig cookies!

While our St. Nicolas does not hail from Bari as does San Nicola, he is a jolly rotund fellow clad in red and fur with rosy cheeks, who delivers rather large gifts.

La Befana is a skinny bedraggled old woman who silently brings gifts to Italian children on the twelfth day of Christmas. That is the feast of the Epiphany, the day the three wise men, after following the star, arrived at the manger in Bethlehem to adore the infant Jesus.

She too, is magical, invisible, and silent with a bag full of small toys for girls and boys.

135

They celebrate Christmas twice in Italy, first on December 25th then on January 6th. I like the idea of two days to get gifts and eat well. I try to have a family gathering on January 6th, an Epiphany party, to celebrate the closure of the season. The ulterior motive is to finish up the leftover cookies and to have my children help take down the tree and carry the ornaments to the attic.

I still enjoy one of my favorite Christmas poems entitled La Befana, (author unknown.)

Zitti, zitti presto a letto	Quiet, quiet, quickly get to bed
La Befana è qui sul tettto	La Befana is here on the roof
Sta guardando dal camino	She is watching through the chimney
Se già dorme ogni bambino,	If all the children are asleep
Se la calza è ben appesa	If the stocking is hung right
Se la luce è ancora accesa	If the light is still on
Quando scende ?	When will she come down?
Appena è sola	As soon as she is alone
Svelti, sotto alle lenzuola!	Quickly get under the sheets
Li chiudete o no quegli occhi?	Will you shut those eyes?
Se non siete più che buoni	If you are not good
Niente dolci o balocchi	No sweets or toys
Solo cenere e carboni	Only ashes and coal.

I never got coal and we didn't have a fireplace when I was little. But we had a skylight and Santa managed to find me anyway to deliver my usual gifts- the yearly pajamas, a book, a game or even a bracelet. Now, Santa Claus brings too many gifts. There is mass confusion as we open presents. I don't remember what I gave or what I receive but I love Christmas anyway. With global shrinking Babbo Natale does visit some homes in Italy but I don't think La Befana comes to New York yet.

I think it would be fun to go to Italy right after New Year's Day. I would be just in time to get gifts all over again on the Epiphany. I might still catch the *zampognari* (bagpipers) in the streets, and eat some roasted chestnuts in a piazza. I could see the decorations, visit the presepio at the Vatican and might catch a glimpse of La Befana flying on her broomstick over the Tiber river in Rome.

As Santa Claus says after he gives his team a whistle and flies away,"Happy Christmas to all and to all a good night." La Befana says, "Buon Anno a tutti!"

RINASCIMENTO

In the cycle of seasons, Spring is the time of rebirth. Dogwood and cherry trees bloom and tulips, daffodils and hyacinths that have made it through the winter burst through the ground in a colorful greeting to the new season. When I see chicks, ducklings and baby rabbits in pet store windows, I know Easter is approaching.

Years ago, I bought the live Easter symbols for my children (before the cruelty to animal laws were enacted). We had six newly hatched chicks one year. My children gave them creative names like Pancake, Doodle, and Gregory. They took very good care of their delicate pets keeping them clean, and feeding them "spaghetti" worms.

They grew quickly and started to jump out of their cardboard box and run around the basement. When we started to smell them upstairs we knew it was time to put them outside in a wire enclosure. The growing chicks were a big hit with all the neighborhood kids.

All went well until a phone call woke me up one morning. I sleepily said "Hello," and all I heard was a loud "COCK A DOODLE DOO" in my ear! Two of our six chicks had grown up to be roosters who crowed "Buon Giorno" at sunrise! The neighbors thought I should be awake as well.

When our town had a pet show, our beautiful brown rooster redeemed himself and won first prize, a blue ribbon for most unusual pet! Although Gregory turned out to be a hen, she never laid eggs. Later we had to donate the chickens to a farm.

One year my children couldn't resist the baby rabbits at a petting farm. So we bought a quiet soft white bunny and named her Penelope. She went to school for "show and tell" and somehow we acquired another rabbit, floppy eared Clyde. And in the season of rebirth we soon had a bunch of mixed breed little rabbits. Penelope met with a sad fate though. One night a pack of stray dogs attacked the outdoor hutch. Barking awakened us and we threw shoes and called the police, but we could not save our bunnies.

We had an empty hutch until someone gave us "April", a sweet docile Dutch bunny who was happy just munching on lettuce. April had some adventures also. Once she fell in the canal behind my house. My youngest son jumped in to rescue her before we discovered rabbits can actually swim. Another time a friend's mutt sniffed our little cottontail. Trying to escape, April circled our house with lightening speed. She was winning the race when the dog was finally restrained. Then April collapsed from exhaustion.

The ducklings we had were the easiest Easter pets. They waddled around our yard on their webbed feet and swam in an old children's pool. One day they just joined the Mallards and swans on the canal. For many years they responded to our clicking call, hopped onto our dock and in line formation marched up the ramp to our backyard. They quacked for their dinner- pasta worms and Italian bread, then went back to the water and swam away.

We were lucky our ducklings all turned out to be white Peking ducks. Someone I know had a gosling in their flock and it grew up to be a long necked goose that hissed and snapped at everyone.

These Easter pets were playful THEN, but my advice NOW is to stick to chocolate bunnies, marshmallow "peeps" and plush lavender and yellow ducklings! They are a lot less trouble with no crowing, no quacking and no Peter Cottontail in the vegetable garden. *Buona Pasqua!*

THE BABY LAMB

Pasqua means Easter. Primavera means Spring. For most young people today those words have a new concept- "Spring Break" in Mexico or Florida!

Long ago the Easter season was a time of reflection and religious observance. It started on Fat Tuesday when a funny "chocolate pudding" appeared in Italian bakery showcases and we were obliged to taste "sanguinaccio"(blood pudding). We had a last heavy meat meal and played jokes on family members as a Carnevale tradition brought over from the towns in Italy. The next day, Ash Wednesday, started a fast for the forty days of Lent. Somehow liver and spinach were easy to give up but after five days we couldn't live without cake or candy.

I try to maintain holiday customs TODAY but my parents had a unique Easter tradition that would be hard for me to repeat.

Every year they received a "baby lamb" as a gift from relatives who had a farm in Highland New York. It was an honor to receive this gift. It was alive!

This "baby lamb" became the family pet for my nieces and nephews. Each day they would hurry home from school with friends and go directly into the garage to feed and play with it. A few days before Easter SOMEHOW the "little lamb" ran away. They searched everywhere, even at school, but it was not found. After many questions and tears the children were appeased and all was forgotten by Easter Sunday.

During Holy Week, we looked forward to our Holy Thursday pilgrimage to an odd number of churches. Priests blessed our homes and on Venerdì Santo we did not listen to the radio and most of the day was spent in church for the washing of the feet ritual. Then the purple shrouds that covered the statues and made the church look spooky, were removed, and on Easter Sunday the church rejoiced and burst into color with lilies, tulips, and Spring flowers.

At home, a sumptuous meal was prepared. After the antipasto and ravioli came "Capretto" the Easter delicacy.

When my oldest nephew was about nine years old, he became enlightened. He blurted out, "That's our baby lamb!" Gasps of horror came from five children. What had been called a "baby lamb" was in reality a kid, a baby goat! It had been sacrificed and was our Easter specialty "capretto."

None of the children ate their holiday meal that year and probably don't eat lamb to this day. They wouldn't eat the lamb shaped cake with white icing, coconut "wool" and a blue ribbon collar either.

I don't think any part of the goat was wasted because we ate capozella including the brain and eye. We had soffritto, a stew of innards, and the intestines made skewered "stigghioli": all parts of our little gift. I know I could not tolerate having any of that today.

Our Easter celebration also included coloring eggs that were then baked into bread twists or large cookies called "pupi con uova." Most families made a wonderful homemade grain and ricotta pie for dessert. Today the peace dove "la colomba" cake is also popular. Rather than bunnies we had large chocolate eggs wrapped with fluffy paper. Each egg had a prize inside. Last year Perugina said they had a diamond ring in one egg. I didn't get that one.

Every Easter I think of the little goat story and if I'm in a restaurant I order ham! *Buona Pasqua* everyone.

Is this a baby lamb or a *capretto*?

140

SANTA'S GIFT

I think every child wants to get a puppy for Christmas. That's when Mom and Dad's guard is weakened and the Christmas spirit takes over. When one of my sons insisted that Santa would surely bring him a live puppy, I had to relent. My allergy story had become old and while Santa was still a visitor on Christmas Eve, what could I do? I finally had to consent.

We went to the animal shelter on the day before Christmas and picked the cutest mixed breed puppy - a sad eyed part beagle, part dachshund with a wagging tail who had just been weaned from its mother. The poor puppy whimpered all Christmas Eve but when my children saw her at 5 AM Christmas morning she wagged her tail. My children jumped and shouted with glee and it was worth it. All the other gifts were temporarily ignored.

We went through the agony of naming this puppy for days. We tried names like Santa, Jingles, Clausy, even "Natale" but settled on Jinglebell. Then a friend said,

"You're Italian. You should give your dog an Italian name."

So we added an "a" to make it "Jinglebella!"

Some relatives called her Jingle Brutta because she became the terror of the neighborhood barking at anything that moved within 100 feet of our house.

Her name fit her. Her collar jingled when she met us at the front door and she preferred Italian cuisine. She rejected canned dog food for our pasta, and leftovers. She would position herself under the table at dinner time to receive anything that was passed down to her- including eggplant or beans. My sons insisted she smiled at them but, perhaps it was indigestion!

Many Italian Americans do pay tribute to their heritage by extending Italian names to their pets. My daughter's Dalmatian is called Tosca, from Verdi's opera. A friend has purring cats called Tina and Toni - or officially Pastina and Rigatoni! I also know a Tabby named Positano. When I was a kid, we had a dog named "Rex" (Latin for "king ") who lived outside and was really a watch dog for my father's store. Rex didn't get along with our inside cat named Nini. Later we had a kitten named Concetta.

The Christmas day that Santa delivered Jinglebella, was one of the happiest Christmases ever. Every year after that she had a stocking hung on the fireplace, just like the humans in the family. That pup became an integral part of my children's formative years. Jinglebella gave us a litter of six puppies (fathered by the dog down the block) and fourteen years of pleasure <u>except</u> when she bit the paper boy, and when she had to be sprayed with mace by the mailman, or when she became carsick. My four children never became ill in the car but we had to have a dog that needed Dramamine to travel to the veterinarian.

When the kids when off to college and the dog died, we had to start a new phase of life. Despite the bother she caused at times, we think she must have earned her way into doggie paradise. We should have had her cloned because we still miss her.

Merry Christmas Jinglebella and Buon Natale everybody.

Jinglebella.

CHRISTMAS ALL YEAR LONG

I try to start my Christmas shopping while traveling in Italy-even if it is July. I am coaxed into counting the days until Christmas when I admire Rafaello's celestial Madonna and Child paintings in the churches and museums.

On my recent visit to the Basilica of Saint Francis in Assisi, I marveled at the Giotto frescoes that date back to the 1300's. They miraculously survived the earthquake of 1997. Once you see Giotto's blue sky in "The Flight into Egypt" with Mary on a donkey and St Joseph walking beside her you can never forget it.

Centuries ago, wealthy families and nobles commissioned paintings for their private chapels. Fra Filippo Lippi, painted beautiful angels, and Piero della Francesca, Signorelli, Perugino, used the nativity tableau to create many masterpieces depicting the Annunciation, the Holy Family, or the Adoration. The background landscape sometimes showed identifiable family towers that certainly were not in Bethlehem. Now, some of these paintings are renowned and are on our Christmas cards and postage stamps.

In New York City, it is not Christmas for me until I visit the Metropolitan Museum of Art and the majestic Christmas tree. It is festooned with Neapolitan baroque angels and cherubs. The handmade creche dates back to the 1700's in Naples.

While some families set up train sets or snow villages, I set up my *presepio*. I love the Italian tradition of displaying the nativity in the home at Christmastime. I am thankful that my manger figures are made of olive wood and are not fragile. The camels are usually misiing when my grandchildren rearrange the statuettes. As I place Jesus, Joseph, and Mary, and The Three Wise Men in my manger, I remember the baby Jesus my grandmother brought from Italy many yeas ago. When you opened the box it played *Tu Scendi dalle Stelle*, and the head turned and looked at you. It impressed me when I was a child.

Churches here display a manger in December but the nativity scene is very important in Italian towns. You can see a permanent *presepio* in a chapel in Taormina or a creche in a glass-enclosed doorway in Urbino, all year long. My surprise was to find an elaborate diorama of the holy scene among the rocks in a cave at Piedigrotta, Calabria.

The many paintings of the "Adoration of the Magi" with the Holy Family, shepherds, and animals usually show the Three Kings, Gaspar, Melchior (my father's name) and Balthasar presenting gifts of gold, frankincense, and myrrh. Since I am always looking for gift suggestions, I am easily influenced and I think, *Those are nice gifts.* I decide on gifts of jewelry and rather than incense or myrrh, I opt for Chanel NO.5 at the duty free shop!

Although I am restricted to things that fit in my suitcase, I try to buy gifts that are lasting. In Italy, they say that frivolous gifts do not last until the feast of *Santo Stefano,* that is December 26! So, I buy silk ties, scarves and gold. Good things come in small packages anyway.

Our Italian *presepio* Christmas tradition is a beautiful and meaningful one. While Rudolph and snowmen are very nice, Christmas is really all about *Gesù Bambino. Buon Natale.*

Where are the camels?